THE
DAMBUSTERS

AND THE EPIC WARTIME RAIDS OF 617 SQUADRON

Bernard Massey.
q. 617. Tiger Force.

G.L (Johny) Johnson
97 ~ 617

THE MILITARY GALLERY COMMEMORATIVE COLLECTION

GRIFFON INTERNATIONAL

THE
DAMBUSTERS
AND THE EPIC WARTIME RAIDS OF 617 SQUADRON

THE PAINTINGS OF THE MILITARY GALLERY

Many of the images featured in this book have been reproduced as limited edition prints by the Military Gallery.

www.militarygallery.com

ISBN 978-0-9549970-7-6
A GRIFFON INTERNATIONAL BOOK

First published in the United Kingdom in 2017 by Griffon International Limited,
2 Station Approach, Wendover, Buckinghamshire, HP22 6BN

APPROACH TO THE MÖHNE by Anthony Saunders ▶

BREACHING THE EDER DAM by Robert Taylor

Lancaster AJ-N climbs hard as their Upkeep bomb explodes
behind them to breach the Eder Dam.

CONTENTS

CONTENTS

BOMB AWAY! ▶
by Robert Taylor

As enemy flak and tracer illuminate the night sky, Guy Gibson attempts to draw the fire as Mick Martin holds
Lancaster AJ-P steady for the release of its Upkeep bomb against the Möhne Dam.

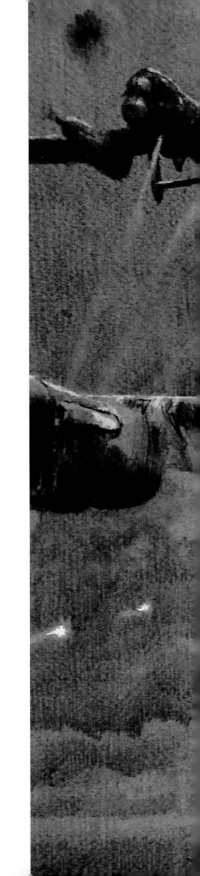

OPERATION CHASTISE by Robert Taylor

The Möhne Dam is finally breached in the early hours of 17 May 1943. Dinghy Young and the crew of
Lancaster AJ-A climb away from the dam as Mick Martin and Guy Gibson bravely circle the flak positions.

INTRODUCTION

Probably as many books have been written about the Dambusters and 617 Squadron as any other aviation subject from World War II. They include works from skilled historians such as John Sweetman, whose research into events are deep and enlightening, as well as established authors like Paul Brickhill, whose words are informative and highly moving. Very few photographs of *Operation Chastise*, however, exist. Less than half a dozen are thought to survive and those that do were taken on the ground at Scampton. It has therefore been left to a handful of talented artists to provide us with a visual record of events.

Over the past forty years 24 survivors of the Dambusters Raid, together with numerous veterans from later 617 Squadron operations, have worked closely with the Military Gallery, themselves pioneers of the aviation art genre. This close association has given our artists, including Robert Taylor, the most famous of them all, an unprecedented insight into the veterans' wartime experiences and allowed them to hear first-hand how operations unfolded, enabling them to create a subjective, yet accurate, pictorial version of the facts.

The result of all these endeavours is the unparalleled collection of paintings and drawings featured in this book. Retrieved from the archives of the Military Gallery they have now been gathered together to tell the amazing story of the Dambusters and 617 Squadron during World War II through art.

We hope the paintings, drawings and maps contained within these pages pay tribute to the memories of all who served with 617 Squadron.

PART ONE

THE GATHERING STORM

TWIST OF FATE
by Richard Taylor

Shortly before the war Adolf Hitler's personal pilot Hans Baur flies the Führer's Ju-52 through the Ruhr valley en-route to the Krupp factories in Essen.

BERLIN
January 1933

When Woodrow Wilson, President of the United States, optimistically declared the Great War of 1914–18 to be "the war that will end all wars", it was not to be. The peace treaty signed at Versailles had led not to a return of sanity but to uncertainty. With the victorious Allies, particularly the French, demanding that the defeated enemy bear the 'full cost of the war', cede territory and disarm most of its military, resentment simmered across Germany.

Then, within a few years of the guns falling silent, a worldwide recession resulted in crashing markets, the fragile German economy descended into ruin and hyperinflation took hold. Whilst communists, socialists, anarchists and nationalists battled for power, one man seized his moment – Adolf Hitler.

Captivated by his charismatic oratory, Hitler's far-right National Socialist German Worker's Party, the Nazi Party, became the largest party in the Reichstag and on 30 January 1933 Hitler was named Chancellor. Within weeks of his appointment fire had destroyed the Reichstag, an event that Hitler blamed on the Communists in opposition; an ailing President Hindenburg was persuaded to declare a state of emergency. Hitler now assumed total power and, banning all other political parties, the Nazis were in full control. With the death of Hindenburg in August 1934 Hitler appointed himself *Führer*. The re-arming of Germany was about to begin whilst in war-weary Britain thoughts of another war began to grow.

On 7 March 1936 armed German troops marched into the Rhineland, previously demilitarised after the Great War. Two years later Austria was annexed, followed by the Sudetenland, the German-speaking region of western Czechoslovakia.

Initially slow to react against the growing threat, Britain introduced its own programme of modernisation and, with war against Germany growing ever more likely, the Air Ministry began to draw up a list of potential strategic targets should the worst happen and war break out. Amongst the targets were the great dams of the Ruhr and Weser that held back the vast reservoirs that fed water into Germany's industrial and manufacturing heartland. If these could be destroyed it could deal a massive blow to the enemy war machine.

THE AIR MINISTRY, London
July 1938

Three dams were chosen as primary targets: the Möhne, the Sorpe and the Eder.

The curving dam across the River Möhne, a tributary of the River Ruhr, lay 25 miles east of Dortmund and was one of the largest dams in Europe. At maximum capacity its wall held back just under 140 million cubic metres of water. Nine miles south-west of the Möhne dam, on the River Sorpe, another tributary of the Ruhr, a second dam held back another 70 million cubic metres. Constructed straight across the river from earth around a concrete core it was, for many years, one of the highest earth dams in the world. The Möhne and Sorpe dams supplied industrial water to the heavy industries and munitions factories of the Ruhr and domestic water to its cities, and helped generate some of the electricity to run the mills, lathes and plants that supplied much of the matériel needed to feed the German war machine.

About forty miles away to the south-east the third dam was on the River Eder, a tributary of the Weser whose lake, containing just over 200 million cubic metres, was the largest reservoir in Europe. The Eder dam also generated hydro-electricity for the energy-guzzling industries but its main functions were to supply water to the important Mittelland Canal, and to regulate the flow of the water into the River Fulda, preventing flooding. If the Eder were breached its vast store of water would inundate the low-lying land downstream, especially around the city of Kassel.

Should the attacks on all three primary targets be successful, three other dams were added as secondary objectives. These were the Ennepe dam situated in the

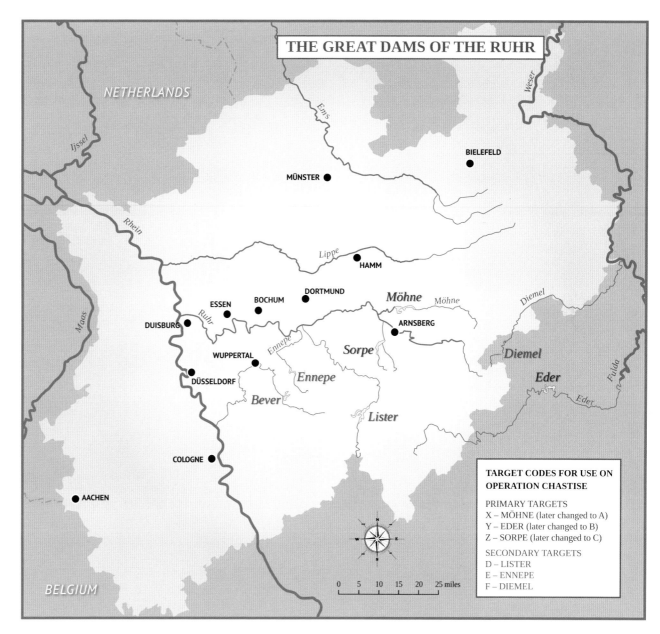

hills 23 miles south-west of Dortmund, the Lister dam north of Dortmund three and a half miles south-east of Lüdenscheid, and the Diemel dam 30 miles away from Kassel and to the north-west of the Eder.

All six, however, had one thing in common – the best time to attack any of them would be during the spring when, with water levels at their highest, it would give Upkeep the best chance of damaging the dam wall sufficiently enough to cause a major breach. Gravity would then help ensure maximum destruction.

At dawn on 1 September 1939 Germany invaded Poland, and Britain and France, obligated by treaty to defend Poland, found themselves once again at war with Germany. The need for a means of destroying these targets now became a reality.

THE GENIUS OF BARNES WALLIS

The means to destroy these targets began when the mind of a genius converged with the aspirations of the various committees, sub-committees and individuals that had identified the dams as targets in the first place. If the dams were to be destroyed it would need a new weapon to do so and one man had been working on such a weapon. His name was Barnes Wallis and for the rest of the war his name and the weapons he designed would be indelibly linked.

Barnes Wallis was already known as a brilliant designer who had worked on the Airship R100. The geodetic construction, developed from work to constrain the airship's gas bags, would provide the main structural element for the construction of the Wellesley and Wellington bombers. Widely respected amongst his peers, at the outbreak of war he was the Assistant Chief Designer at Vickers-Armstrong's Aviation Section, based at Weybridge in Surrey.

It was now that Barnes Wallis turned his attention to bombs. One of these was Upkeep, the codename given to the cylindrical, hydrostatic bomb he invented for the destruction of the Ruhr dams. Upkeep was a masterpiece but there was a problem: for the bomb to work effectively it must be dropped according to a set of highly taxing criteria, such as speed and height. The flying skills needed to do the job would need to be exceptional.

In both the Air Ministry and the Admiralty clever minds had long grappled with the problems of how to attack a dam, and until Upkeep arrived no suitable method had been found. The Admiralty, for example, had been working on a modified air-launched surface-skimming torpedo for use against ships at anchor like the *Tirpitz*. It was an idea that could, perhaps, be adapted for use against a dam but existing aircraft, such as the Blenheim or Hampden, had neither the range nor capability for such low-level operations, as the fate of many aircrews earlier in the war could testify. And when the Germans strung a double row of protective anti-torpedo steel nets across the water in front of the dams, the torpedo method came to nought.

But with the arrival of Upkeep there was now a chance, albeit remote, because to deliver such a weapon with the accuracy and precision needed would require a squadron in which every crew had outstanding flying skills. No such squadron, however, existed and so on 21 March 1943, for the first and only time in Bomber Command's history, a new squadron was formed for a single operation.

Cherry-picking crews from other squadrons, most were highly experienced; some, however, were not. But all had one thing in common, a talent for flying. The task of forming the new unit – to be known as 617 Squadron and part of 5 Group – was given to Wing Commander Guy Gibson.

MARBLES ON THE TERRACE

Barnes Wallis and family in early 'bouncing bomb' experiments, April 1942.

UPKEEP – THE BOUNCING BOMB

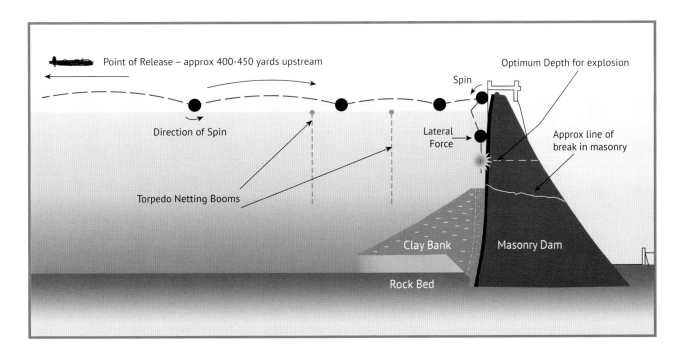

Point of Release – approx 400-450 yards upstream

Direction of Spin

Torpedo Netting Booms

Spin

Lateral Force

Optimum Depth for explosion

Approx line of break in masonry

Clay Bank

Masonry Dam

Rock Bed

Back-spinning the 'bouncing bomb' was, like so many great inventions, the result of a moment of genius when Barnes Wallis realised that back-spinning could not only bounce it over any defensive anti-torpedo nets but increase its speed and range and, most importantly, ensure that when the bomb hit the dam wall the back-spinning would result in the bomb rebounding and crawling down the wall before being detonated at precisely the required point by a depth-sensitive fuse.

Tests showed that to detonate at a point to cause maximum destructive impact the 'bouncing bomb' must contain 6,600lbs of explosive, be released from a height of exactly 60ft some 400-450 yards from the target, and at an airspeed of 210mph. Only one aircraft in the world could carry such a load and perform in these conditions – Bomber Command's latest addition – Avro's magnificent four-engine Lancaster.

THE DAMBUSTERS
A SQUADRON IS BORN

'But I have to warn you that this is no ordinary sortie. In fact it can't be done for at least two months. Moreover', the AVM said, 'the Commander-in-Chief has decided that a special squadron is to be formed for the job. I want you to form that squadron'.

Air Vice-Marshal the Hon Ralph Cochrane AOC 5 Group

These were the words that greeted Guy Gibson on 18 March 1943 as he walked into the AOC's office at 5 Group Headquarters in Grantham. Aged only 24 but already highly decorated with a DSO and DFC and Bar, Gibson had just flown his last tour as Commanding Officer of 106 Squadron. It had been his 71st bomber mission and came at the end of three full tours. Now, instead of leave, he'd been summoned to Grantham.

The question from the Group's new Commanding Officer – the Honourable Ralph Cochrane – met with an immediate 'yes' from Gibson. He was told little and wondered whether this 'no ordinary sortie' was to be the *Tirpitz*. Apart from helping to choose the crews and being informed his base of operations would be at nearby RAF Scampton, his main instruction was that for the next two months they must practise low-level night flying constantly.

"From all over the world they had come: from Australia, America, Canada, New Zealand and Great Britain. All of their own free will. All of them with one idea: to get to grips with the enemy. As I stood there talking to them and drinking beer with them I felt very proud; surely these were the best boys in the world."

Guy Gibson (Enemy Coast Ahead)

RAF SCAMPTON

The village of Scampton lies just to the west of the main A15 trunk road that runs north from nearby Lincoln. Once part of Ermine Street, the great Roman road that linked London to York, it slices purposefully through the fertile countryside where, during the First World War, the village had grown used to the sound of Sopwith Camels and Pups based on the new airfield sandwiched between village and road.

With the Armistice the station had closed. The airmen had departed, taking their aircraft with them. But it wasn't for long: with military developments in Germany taking a worrying course, in 1936 the air force once more returned to Scampton.

On 21 March 1943, the first elements of the new squadron arrived at the base, including Gibson, and over the following few days the aircrew had assembled. They came from across the Dominions: as well as Britons there were Australians, New Zealanders and Canadians, including pilot Joe McCarthy, an American serving in the RCAF.

Original drawing by Richard Taylor

CROSS-COUNTRY by Richard Taylor

In the weeks leading up to Operation Chastise, 617 Squadron were to spend many hours
of low-level flight training criss-crossing the length and breadth of England.

Guy Gibson and his crew in Lancaster AJ-G get airborne from Scampton.

TRAINING AND MORE TRAINING
BUT FOR WHAT?

Nobody on the squadron knew, not even Gibson. The target for their innumerable hours of low-level flying training remained top secret. That's not to say that speculation was rife, with rumours of attacking the battleship *Tirpitz* being the favourite.

The crews now spent two months training to fly at 100ft – less than the wingspan of the aircraft they were flying in – first by day and then by night. They traversed the length and breadth of the country, hedge-hopping over fields, flying under power lines, evading pylons, church steeples, factory chimneys and trees along the way. At the bombing range at Wainfleet they practised bombing runs flying at a speed of 220mph at precisely 60ft. As existing altimeters were incapable of giving such a low reading a system of two downward shining Aldis spotlights,

'My initial reaction was: 'My God, do these things actually fly?!' The first thing you noticed was that it looked like it had had its guts ripped out. There was no bomb bay, just two strange prongs poking down.'
George 'Johnny' Johnson DFM

TOPPING UP SPIRITS by Richard Taylor

As a tanker re-fuels one of 617 Squadron's aircraft, Wing Commander Guy Gibson and his faithful Labrador 'Nigger' share a quiet moment together.

operated by the navigator was devised to converge at exactly 60ft off the surface of the ground. This wasn't normal low-level flying, it was ultra low-level airmanship of the highest order.

George 'Johnny' Johnson, the Bomb-Aimer with American Joe McCarthy's crew, recalled one encounter: *"Then, on one trip, we were on our way home from Wainfleet, barrelling along at, as I recall, not much more* *than 60ft (it might have been a little higher but certainly not more than 100ft) when I got the shock of my life as another Lanc flew underneath us! I was close enough to see their tail gunner waving… it was Les Munro."*

No. 5 GROUP RAF BOMBER COMMAND

By the time 617 Squadron was formed, the Group to which it had been allocated was already one of the most highly regarded in Bomber Command. None other than Air Chief Marshal Arthur Harris, the future Air Officer Commanding-in-Chief for the whole of Bomber Command, had led 5 Group for the first 14 months of the war, a period in which two of the Group's airmen had been awarded the Victoria Cross – Flt Lt Rod Learoyd of 49 Squadron, and Air Gunner Sgt John Hannah from 83 Squadron, both equipped with Hampdens.

Air Vice-Marshal the Honourable Ralph Cochrane, a close friend and associate of Harris, assumed command of 5 Group on 28 February 1943 and once the decision had been taken to form a completely new squadron for the attack on the dams, it came as little surprise that it was to 5 Group that it was allocated.

617 Squadron remained as part of 5 Group for the duration of the war.

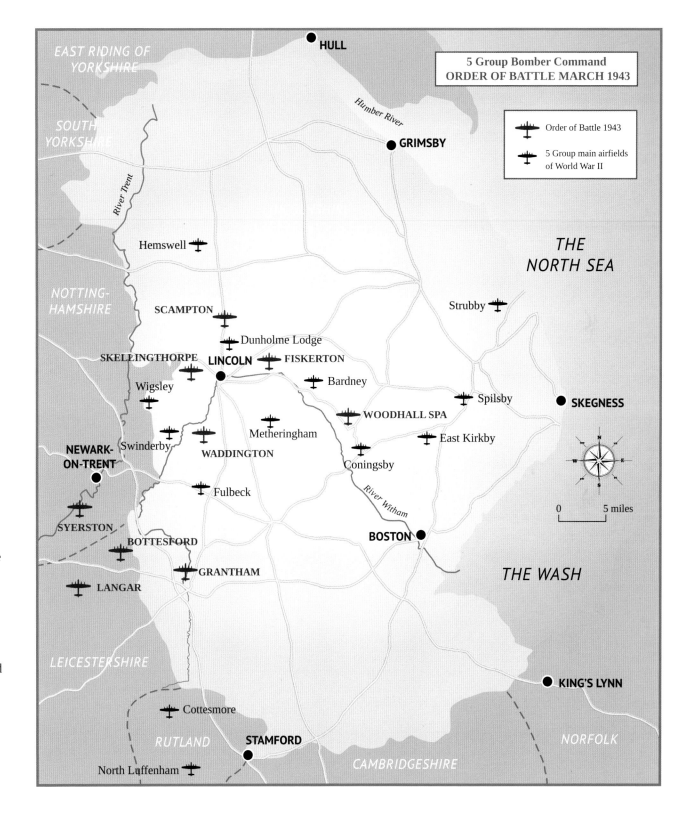

**5 Group Bomber Command
ORDER OF BATTLE MARCH 1943**

Order of Battle 1943

5 Group main airfields of World War II

PART TWO

OPERATION CHASTISE

RAF SCAMPTON
15 May 1943

For the first time Gibson, in the company of Barnes
Wallis, revealed the targets to four men: his two flight
commanders, Henry Melvin 'Dinghy' Young and Henry
Maudslay; his deputy for the attack on the Möhne dam,
John 'Hoppy' Hopgood; and finally Bob Hay who, as
'Mick' Martin's bomb-aimer was to act as the operation's
Bombing Leader. All were sworn to total secrecy.

RAF SCAMPTON
16 May 1943 18.30 hrs

Shortly after mid-day Gibson called all his pilots
and navigators together and finally disclosed their targets
whilst, at the same time, 5 Group's Senior Signals
Officer, Wg Cdr W Dunn, briefed the wireless operators.
Again, all were ordered to keep what they had just been
told completely to themselves. After both briefings
concluded it was late the same afternoon that the simplest

of calls rattled over the Scampton tannoy system:
"All crews of 617 Squadron to report to the briefing
room – immediately."

It was a warm day and the upstairs room, packed to
overflowing with nineteen Lancaster crews, was hot and
stuffy as they sat and waited. But no-one could fail to
notice the models, and the charts and maps on the walls.
As George 'Johnny' Johnson later remarked "...*and
at last the penny dropped. We were to be attacking the*

dams". The significance of the briefing rose further when Gibson arrived and strode towards a raised platform. With him was Air Vice-Marshal the Honourable Ralph Cochrane, the austere AOC of 5 Group, Group Captain John Whitworth, Scampton's Station Commander and a kindly-looking, middle-aged civilian. Most of those present already knew his name – Barnes Wallis.

Addressing the hushed room Gibson opened proceedings by simply announcing that tonight they were going to 'attack the great dams of the Ruhr'. Even though the maps, models and charts were on display, Gibson's bold statement drew an involuntary intake of breath from those not yet briefed. No one in the room needed to be told just how dangerous this operation was going to be.

Barnes Wallis then addressed them in his quiet patrician way to explain about Upkeep: what it was, how it worked and how it came to be built. He explained precisely why intense precision was needed to drop their weapon, the effect it would have on the dam wall, and the reasons why. It was quite unlike a normal briefing as they listened intently, impressed by his quietly spoken words. AVM Cochrane then said a few words and handed over to Gibson who, with the aid of the maps, photographs and models, explained the detailed information of the raid ahead – codenamed *Operation Chastise*.

The First Wave would be led by Gibson. It would consist of nine aircraft taking off in three sections at ten-minute intervals. Gibson, Hopgood and Martin would be followed by Young, Astell and Maltby with Maudslay, Knight and Shannon bringing up the rear. Their target was the Möhne dam and should that be breached they would head to the Eder dam. Any aircraft still carrying their Upkeep would go on to the Sorpe dam.

A Second Wave would consist of five Lancasters led by Joe McCarthy. They would leave in single file and, to confuse the Germans over their destination, would fly a different, more northerly route.

A Third Wave, to depart two and a half hours later, was to act as the 'mobile reserve'. It, too, consisted of five aircraft to be flown by Townsend, Anderson, Brown, Ottley and Burpee and they, like the First Wave, would take the shorter southern route.

The briefing concluded at around 19.30hrs and the weeks of training were over. Operation Chastise was, at last, about to begin.

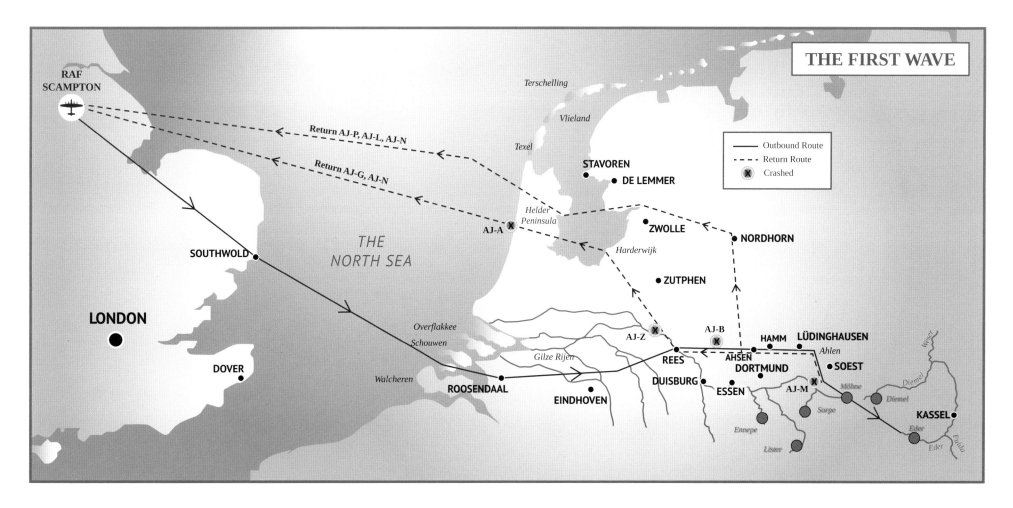

THE DEPARTURE

RAF SCAMPTON
16 May 1943   19.30 hrs

As the briefing ended routine took over and the crews quietly dispersed towards the mess for the customary pre-op supper of bacon and eggs. Unsurprisingly the atmosphere was quieter than usual as the enormity of the night's work ahead sunk in. Tension was mounting but, as before any other operation, time went quickly and soon everyone was changing into their flying kit. Some had written letters, just in case things turned out badly, others had not. Some joked, most were restrained, and some went through rituals known only to themselves. Lucky mascots took their place; Mick Martin stuffed a toy koala bear into his flying jacket whilst Gibson snatched up his 'lucky' Mae West lifejacket taken from a German prisoner earlier in the war. David Maltby took his old scruffy hat and Bill Radcliffe, the Canadian Flight Engineer on Joe McCarthy's crew, tucked a toy panda bear into his flying boot. For him it worked, the little bear would accompany him on more than 60 missions during the war.

Not everything, however, had been lucky. The previous evening Gibson's dog, a much-loved black Labrador retriever called Nigger, had been knocked over and killed by a car just outside Scampton's main gate. The untimely death of the squadron's popular mascot, whose liking for beer was the source of much amusement, had come as a blow to those that heard about it. Nigger had been Gibson's companion since he was a puppy but now all Gibson had time for was to arrange his dog's funeral. He was buried at midnight outside the squadron hangar. It was also the hour at which, with luck, his owner should be crossing the Dutch coast.

"Then I was alone in my room looking at the scratch marks on the door Nigger used to make when he wanted to go out, and feeling very depressed".
Guy Gibson (Enemy Coast Ahead)

Original drawing by Robert Taylor

RAF SCAMPTON
15.30 hrs DISPERSAL

All day and well into evening all of the squadron's available ground crew had worked tirelessly to get 617's nineteen specially modified Lancasters ready and armed for the night's raid. Officially the aircraft were 'Type 464 Provisioning' Lancasters, adapted at Avro's Woodford factory near Macclesfield specifically to carry Barnes Wallis's Upkeep mine. The bomb bay doors had been replaced by fairings, a v-shaped calliper arm fitted on each side to hold Upkeep securely in place, and the mechanism to make it spin. To make way for this the mid-upper turrets had been removed. A pilot from the Ferry Pilot's Pool described them as looking like a 'gutted fish' and there was no doubt that these were some of the oddest-looking Lancasters ever built.

Whatever their shape, however, maintenance teams now swarmed all over them, tuning and re-tuning engines, double-checking flaps, ailerons and every working part to make sure each aircraft ran as faultlessly as possible. Groups of armourers heaved thousands of rounds of daylight tracer into each of the two remaining turrets and all afternoon bowsers kept up a continuous stream from fuel dump to waiting aircraft, delivering the 1,760 gallons of high-octane petrol needed for the flight. And finally, the precious Upkeeps, each weighing 9,000lbs, arrived and were attached.

Everything was ready and all that the aircraft needed now were the crews to fly them.

FINAL BRIEFING by Anthony Saunders

Against a background of fast-receding sunlight Guy Gibson readies his crew before they climb inside their modified Lancaster AJ-G. The other crews will do the same and just before 21.30hrs the first will climb through the fast-fading rays, en-route to attack the mighty dams of the Ruhr.

21.10 hrs DISPERSAL

Kitted out for flying and with parachutes and other equipment issued, the waiting crews took the chocolate, sandwiches and coffee needed for the trip and waited to be called. As each crew was summoned they bundled themselves into the trucks and old buses that would take them out across the airfield to the waiting aircraft out at various dispersal points around Scampton's perimeter. It was now that many got their first glimpse of Upkeep. All were suitably impressed by its size.

Against a background of receding sunlight the captains of the first two waves gave their crews a final briefing before climbing inside their Lancasters to prepare and wait for the signal to start engines. It came at 21.10hrs – a red Very light that curled lazily into the sky fired by Bob Hutchison, Gibson's Wireless Operator.

Within minutes the airfield was pulsating with the thunder of 56 Merlin engines warming to operating temperature.

Original drawing by Robert Taylor

Original drawing by Richard Taylor

RAF SCAMPTON
21.28 hrs PERIMETER TRACK

One by one the five Lancasters of the Second Wave lumbered forward, their tyres rolling slowly over the hard ground as the pitch of the engines increased to move the heavily-laden aircraft. Having the longest route to fly, the Second Wave would be the first to get airborne and it wasn't long before they were in position with Scampton's grass runway before them and a green Aldis lamp flashed from the control caravan. It was time to get Operation Chastise underway.

Flt Lt Bob Barlow took a deep breath and pushed open the throttles of AJ-E to maximum and the Lancaster rolled forward, increasing speed as it slowly gathered pace over the grass. It was going to be tight but at last Barlow heaved back on the stick and they were airborne.

In his cramped rear turret Sgt Jack Liddell unknowingly took his last view of Scampton, fast receding into the distance.

21.39 hrs PERIMETER TRACK

With the Second Wave all safely off the ground and on their way, at 21.39hrs the green lamp flashed again. It was time for Gibson's main force of nine aircraft to depart, which they did in style, in a vic of three formation. Gibson led, flanked by Hopgood and Martin in a broad vic. Eight minutes later Young, Maltby and Shannon left and finally, at 21.59hrs, Maudslay, Astell and Knight completed the First Wave's departure. For those on the ground the air fell uncannily silent.

The reserve crews of the Third Wave now had a tense, unenviable two hour wait.

It was just possible they wouldn't be needed but, there again, perhaps they might.

Original drawing by Robert Taylor

GREEN ON GO by Robert Taylor

Lancasters of 617 Squadron taxi along the perimeter track
prior to their departure from Scampton.

THE FIRST WAVE
EN-ROUTE

As the First Wave climbed over the perimeter fence and away from Scampton they immediately banked and skimmed low over the Wash, heading south-east. The last rays of the setting sun continued to diminish as they made their way towards the Suffolk coast, which they crossed over the once-popular pre-war resort of Southwold whose distinctive Victorian pier, partially dismantled in 1940 for fear of invasion, was clearly visible.

Now, as they headed out across the North Sea towards the enemy coast, Gibson and the others dropped even lower to avoid enemy detection. Flying at wave-top height it was time for them to set their altimeters at 60ft, a height which they and the crews following must now maintain all the way to the target.

The crews were used to the dangers of flak and enemy night-fighters. They'd encountered them before and knew what to expect – not that it made things any easier – but the perils to be encountered by flying at such low-levels were going to test the pilots' skills to the extreme.

PATHWAY TO THE RUHR by Anthony Saunders

With silver moonlight glinting on the wave tops below, Guy Gibson leads the First Wave of Lancasters across the North Sea heading towards the Dutch coast. In perfect formation with Mick Martin on his port side and Hoppy Hopgood to starboard, the three aircraft have set their altimeters to 60ft and will fly at this height all the way to the target in an effort to avoid enemy detection.

ON COURSE FOR THE MÖHNE DAM
by Richard Taylor

The unmistakable thunder of Merlin engines shatters the night as Guy Gibson leads the First Wave of 617 Squadron's Lancaster bombers across Holland en-route towards Germany. After crossing the coast a fraction off course, Gibson adjusts their compass heading slightly and follows a large canal where the owner of a windmill, hearing the noise, hurries outside to witness the event.

WALCHEREN

Gibson led the First Wave up the dark stretches of the Scheldt estuary and across the Dutch coast at the island of Schouwen, just north of Walcheren where, in eighteen months' time, British commandos would launch an amphibious assault in a blizzard of fire to fight a brave and bloody battle. For now, however, the light of the waxing gibbous moon merely glinted on placid water a few feet below.

Stronger than expected winds had slowed the group and skewed their course a bit but this was spotted and quickly corrected. More importantly, and as hoped, they'd taken the German defences by surprise and only a few balls of random flak, some distance away, had spat out hopefully into the night sky but it was still unknown how long that luck would last. And, even if it held, there was nothing to hide the other dangers that lay en-route: the ever-present threat of colliding with windmills, tall trees and pylons which, with a deadly thread of high-tension power cables strung between them, waited like a spider's web ready to ensnare its prey.

INBOUND TO TARGET
by Robert Taylor

En-route to the Möhne Dam Flight Lieutenant Mick Martin in company with Flight Lieutenant John Hopgood in the distance flew so low over Holland that their wingtips barely missed pylons and the sails of windmills below.

The First Wave follow the Dutch canals en-route to the Möhne Dam.

Original drawing by Richard Taylor

00.19 hrs EN-ROUTE TO TARGET

There was little the gunners could do inside their bumpy turrets, apart from keeping a keen look-out, and several that night were to take full advantage of their low-level situation, squirting bursts of tracer at one or two trains they spotted along the way.

All seemed to be going well. The nine crews were successfully navigating their difficult path along and across the canals of Holland towards the Rhine. But then,

as the last of the three formations crossed the German border, twenty minutes after Gibson's trio, disaster struck.

At 00.15hrs Bill Astell in AJ-B did what they all feared and collided with the top of a pylon. The fully-laden aircraft crashed in a ball of flame and fire. There were no survivors – the First Wave had suffered its first casualties.

Ahead of AJ-B those in Gibson's leading vic were much further east, north of the Ruhr and past Borken

when, at last, the long-awaited German flak batteries opened up with a vengeance. It had been unmarked and, shortly afterwards, the port wing of Hopgood's Lancaster took some undetermined damage. But for all of them attention was clearly focused on what lay ahead because they were now approaching the hills and valleys of the Ruhr – and the target.

Original drawing by Robert Taylor

THE ATTACK ON THE MÖHNE DAM by Richard Taylor

THE MÖHNE DAM

'As we came over the hill, we saw the Möhne Lake. Then we saw the dam itself. In that light it looked squat and unconquerable; it looked grey and solid in the moonlight, as though it were part of the countryside itself and just as immovable.'

Guy Gibson (Enemy Coast Ahead)

G-GEORGE
00.20 hrs THE MÖHNE DAM

Back at Scampton the Third Wave had been called into action and were all airborne shortly before Gibson and his flight crossed the last of the hills surrounding the Möhne lake and saw their target for the first time. Young, Maltby and Shannon in the second flight arrived a few minutes later and the hour of reckoning had finally arrived. Now, not only were their weeks of training to be put to the test but so too was Barnes Wallis' 'bouncing bomb' – Upkeep.

As soon as the bombers came into view the flak positions defending the dam opened up with 20mm and 37mm calibre guns, the night tracer sending streams of yellow, red and green across the lake whilst Gibson slowly circled the area to assess the plan of attack. Checking that everyone had arrived, he called them up only to find that Bill Astell gave no response. Unknown to them his aircraft was already a blazing wreck.

It was, however, time to attack and, as ever, Gibson led from the front and dived, coming in low and wide over the surrounding hills, heading for the dam until the Aldis lights confirmed the surface of the lake was 60ft below. The flak was intense as they skimmed low over the dark waters, but AJ-G was leading a charmed life and miraculously wasn't hit. Their

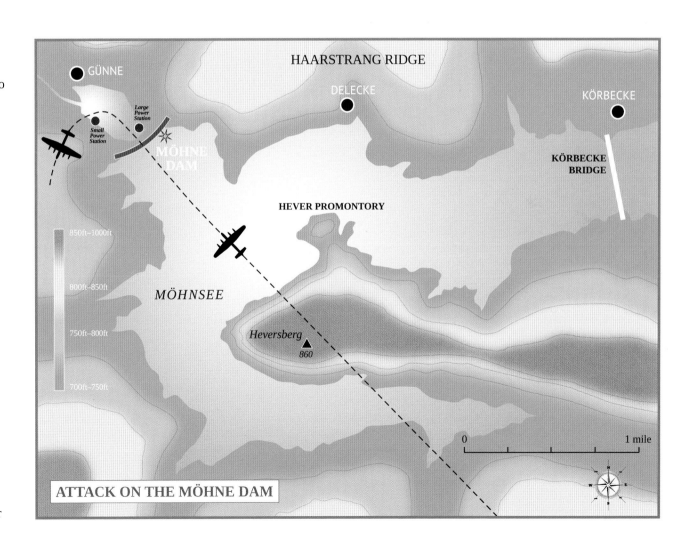

ATTACK ON THE MÖHNE DAM

Upkeep released, Gibson thundered over the dam's wall giving Flt Lt Richard Trevor-Roper in the rear turret a grandstand view as their Upkeep bounced towards the target and, as Gibson banked hard away, everyone on board could see the towering column of water 1,000ft high caused by the huge detonation. The dam held.

Wireless Operator Bob Hutchison transmitted GONER 6 8 A back to Operations HQ: 'Special weapon released, exploded 5yds from dam – no apparent breach – Target A (Möhne).

M-MOTHER
00.20 hrs THE MÖHNE DAM

Disappointed that his mine had failed to make any apparent impression on the dam, Gibson called up his deputy Hoppy Hopgood in AJ-M with the words 'Hello, M-Mother, you may attack now. Good luck'.

'OK, attacking' came the brief reply.

It was the last transmission Hopgood would ever make. As AJ-M approached the dam the flak teams had had all the time they needed to adjust their guns; they knew exactly where the next attack was coming from and threw up a solid wall of fire. AJ-M was badly hit, dragging a long tail of flame behind it and, in all the chaos, their Upkeep was released a fraction too late. Bouncing right over the top of the dam it landed on the power station below and exploded. Hopgood, knowing M-Mother was stricken, struggled to gain altitude in a desperate attempt to allow the crew time to bale out.

Incredibly three did so: John Fraser, the Canadian Bomb-Aimer and Australian Tony Burcher, the Rear

M-MOTHER OVER THE MÖHNE DAM by Robert Taylor

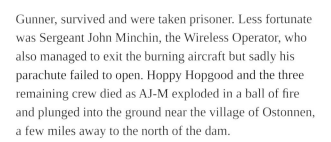

Gunner, survived and were taken prisoner. Less fortunate was Sergeant John Minchin, the Wireless Operator, who also managed to exit the burning aircraft but sadly his parachute failed to open. Hoppy Hopgood and the three remaining crew died as AJ-M exploded in a ball of fire and plunged into the ground near the village of Ostonnen, a few miles away to the north of the dam.

P-POPSIE
00.38 hrs THE MÖHNE DAM

For a brief moment everyone was stunned into silence by the horror of what they had just witnessed. The cruel wreckage of Hopgood's burning Lancaster could be clearly seen and, as leader, it fell to Gibson to take control of the situation and quickly renew the assault. He immediately called up Mick Martin circling in AJ-P Popsie and ordered him to attack. Pilots normally used the call sign P for Peter but Martin, on his first flight in AJ-P had used P for Popsie and it stuck.

Now Popsie's crew, having witnessed the intensity of the flak and Hopgood's resulting tragedy, was in no doubt about the reception awaiting them.

In an act of great courage Gibson, in an effort to draw some of the deadly flak away from Martin, flew alongside and slightly ahead of AJ-P. Martin was the master of low-flying, however, and would earn the reputation of the greatest bomber pilots of war. Flying at low-level was his speciality and no-one could do it better. Although AJ-P was shot up and hit several times as they approached the target, Martin held her steady, flying straight and level whilst his Front Gunner Toby Foxlee,

yelling at the top of his voice, fired a barrage of tracer towards the flak towers across the water.

The plan seemed to work; the German gunners, now forced to split their fire between two targets, gave Martin the run he needed and at 00.38hrs Bomb-Aimer Bob Hay released their spinning Upkeep.

THE DAMBUSTERS by Robert Taylor

As Gibson helps draw away the enemy fire, Mick Martin releases his Upkeep bomb.

Original drawing by Robert Taylor

GONER 58A by Robert Taylor

With Gibson drawing some of the flack, Mick Martin powers his Lancaster AJ-P above the Möhne dam having released his Upkeep.

Tammy Simpson, the Australian Rear Gunner, was too busy spraying his Brownings at the flak positions to watch the great mine bouncing across the water and exploding as the hydrostatic pistol detonated. Once again, as with Gibson's attack, a great column of water hurled itself skywards as everyone looked on expectantly, willing the wall to crack apart.

But, as before, once the boiling cauldron finally subsided back into the lake, it was clear to Gibson, now circling overhead, that the dam wall still held.

Three aircraft had now attacked and time was ticking by as New Zealander Len Chambers, Martin's Radio Operator, tapped out the code for another failure – GONER 5 8 A – 'Special weapon released, exploded 50 yds from dam – no apparent breach – Target A (Möhne)'. In the underground control room at 5 Group HQ in Grantham each 'GONER' was met with dismay, especially by Wallis who sat head in hands, foreseeing disaster. Amidst the tense atmosphere nerves were fraying.

BREACHING THE MÖHNE by Gerald Coulson

Mick Martin's Lancaster climbing away as his Upkeep mine sends a plume of water high into the air behind him. In the distance Gibson attempts to draw some of the flak.

THE IMPOSSIBLE MISSION
by Robert Taylor

There is a huge splash as the Upkeep bomb from Dinghy Young's Lancaster AJ-A hits the water of the Möhne lake.

A-APPLE
00.40 hrs THE MÖHNE DAM

As the water settled Dinghy Young in AJ-A came on the air: 'A-Apple' making bombing run.'

This time Mick Martin joined Gibson in attempting to draw some of the enemy flak away from Young's aircraft, with Gibson flicking on his lights to distract the enemy gunners. Young's bomb was spot on target and Gibson noted that the bomb made 'three good bounces' before detonating against the dam wall. The resulting

LAST MOMENTS OF THE MÖHNE DAM
by Robert Taylor

Dinghy Young clears the parapet of the Möhne Dam
seconds after releasing his bomb.

tower of water spilt into the valley beyond and Young
excitedly called in 'I think I've done it! I've broken it'.

Deep within the dam wall the great blocks of stone
were groaning under the shock of repeated explosions
and, imperceptibly, they were shifting under the stress.

Pressure was mounting within and the dam weakening,
succumbing to the laws of nature that Wallis believed
could destroy it. But the wall was holding – just.

Another 'GONER' message was transmitted back to
Grantham and the air of despondency already over Barnes

Wallis deepened further. For months he and his small
team had battled day and night to ensure that Upkeep
worked but now all he could think of was the lives of
so many young men that were being placed in danger,
perhaps for nothing.

J-JOHNNY
00.49 hrs THE MÖHNE DAM

At the Möhne, however, Gibson felt much more upbeat. Despite the terrible loss of Hopgood and the three failures, he felt sure that the dam was about to give way and that success was almost upon them. During Young's attack Gibson had been flying on the airside of the dam in order to give even more distraction to the gunners, and he was convinced he'd seen the wall move slightly after the explosion. But obviously not enough.

He now called up David Maltby in AJ-J to begin his run-in.

J-Johnny came in low and fast over the Hever promontory, and this time Gibson flew to Maltby's right and Martin to Maltby's left, once again both of them engaging and confusing the enemy gunners whose rate of fire had now diminished. Fortuitously by now one flak gun had jammed and another had been damaged by the explosion of Martin's mine. In desperation some of the German gunners now resorted to rifle fire as J-Johnny

THREE GOOD BOUNCES by Robert Taylor

Lit by the flames of the burning power station below, A-Apple just clears the Möhne Dam as their Upkeep makes 'three good bounces' before striking the dam wall.

THE WALL BEGINS TO CRUMBLE by Richard Taylor

closed on the dam. From his vantage point in the canopy Maltby could clearly see the damage ahead caused by Young's bomb. At 00.49hrs Bomb-Aimer John Fort released their own Upkeep, it bounced to perfection, hit the wall, sank and exploded.

For some reason Sergeant Tony Stone, Maltby's Wireless Operator, didn't wait before transmitting 'GONER 7 8 A' back to Grantham. Another failure. But was it?

Gibson called up Dave Shannon in AJ-L to begin his attack but then it happened; the dam began disintegrating before his eyes, the mighty Möhne Dam had been breached. As he called Shannon off his attack he watched a terrifying tidal wave of water thunder and crash into the valley below. Bob Hutchison, Gibson's wireless operator, began transmitting…

'There was a great breach 100yds across, and the water, looking like stirred porridge in the moonlight, was gushing out and rolling into the Ruhr Valley....'
Guy Gibson (Enemy Coast Ahead)

00.56 hrs 5 GROUP HQ GRANTHAM

At 00.56hrs Hutchison's transmission began to arrive. The Morse chattered out and Wg Cdr Dunn, the Group's Signals Officer, received the letters N-I-G-G-E-R, the code word for a successful breach, before bellowing out 'They've done it!' A shockwave of profound relief swept across the room, in an instant changed from gloom to ecstasy. Wallis leapt from his seat and punched the air as the top brass rushed over to shake his hand and offer their congratulations. Wallis beamed, the burden lifted. Upkeep had worked and the Möhne dam had been breached.

THE BREACH by Anthony Saunders

Lancaster AJ-J, with pilot David Maltby at the controls, banks steeply away after delivering
the coup-de-grâce to the Möhne Dam. The devastation caused by Hopgood's bomb
exploding on the power station is visible below as the huge explosion and towering pillar of
water that marks the breach.

AFTERMATH AT THE MÖHNE

As the seven surviving Lancasters of the First Wave circled overhead, it became apparent that the opening in the dam wall was huge. A gap of more than 300 feet had completely disappeared, the granite blocks swept into oblivion by the torrent of escaping water. Gibson later wrote: "The floods raced on, carrying with them as they went – viaducts, railways, bridges and everything that stood in their path. Three miles beyond the dam the remains of Hoppy's aircraft were still burning gently, a dull red glow on the ground. Hoppy had been avenged."

With the first target destroyed, and conscious that time was passing, Gibson told Martin and Maltby to head home, and made Young his new deputy. With Gibson leading, the surviving crews set course for the Eder.

LOW PASS OVER THE MÖHNE DAM
by Anthony Saunders

Guy Gibson powers over the Möhne dam to confirm the extent of the breach and the swirling torrent of water surging into the valley below.

SCHLOSS WALDECK by Richard Taylor

Low over Schloss Waldeck, Dave Shannon, pilot of Lancaster AJ-L, slowly circles the Eder lake in preparation for his attack on the Eder Dam.

BREACHING THE EDER

Even in daylight, under perfect flying conditions, it would take extraordinary skill to breach the Eder.

High on octane after their success at the Möhne, Gibson's wave arrived at the Eder which, although undefended, was a much more difficult target because of the surrounding topography.

From the surface of the *Ederstausee*, the vast serpentine lake formed behind the dam wall, the dark hills climbed steeply away to a height of over 1,000ft. This was the height the Lancasters had to lose in precious little space whilst undertaking a sharp 90-degree turn and avoiding a wooded spit of land at the same time. Even in daylight, under perfect flying conditions, it would take extraordinary flying skills and nerve to be in the correct position 60ft above the lake and with enough space for the remaining Upkeeps to work. It had seemed daunting enough at the briefing but this was now night and, worryingly, patches of mist were beginning to form in the valleys and spill eerily over the water.

L-LOVE (LEATHER)
01.30 hrs THE EDER DAM

Without wasting any more time reflecting on the difficulties Gibson swiftly ordered David Shannon to make his attack but, after several failed attempts at reaching the correct height, Henry Maudslay in Z-Zebra tried his luck, again without success. It was proving impossible to get in position. Once again Shannon tried and after a couple of attempts finally got his chance, releasing his Upkeep bang on target.

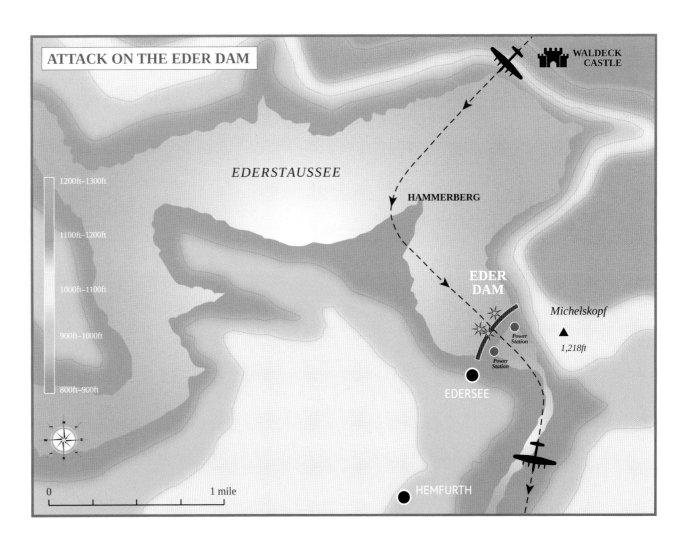

ATTACK ON THE EDER DAM

WALDECK CASTLE

EDERSTAUSSEE

HAMMERBERG

1200ft–1300ft

1100ft–1200ft

1000ft–1100ft

900ft–1000ft

800ft–900ft

EDER DAM

Michelskopf

Power Station

1,218ft

Power Station

EDERSEE

0   1 mile

HEMFURTH

Climbing hard on full power to avoid a collision with the *Michelskopf*, the dangerous high hill beyond the dam, Shannon's crew could see the now familiar towering plume of water from their mine's explosion as it subsided and settled back into the lake. Instinctively Shannon felt that they'd made a small breach and told his wireless operator, Flying Officer Brian Goodale, to transmit GONER 7 9 B – 'Special weapon released, exploded in contact with the dam – small breach – Target B (Eder).

For some unknown reason the message took more than half an hour to arrive at Grantham. When it did finally get through events had changed considerably.

Z-ZEBRA
01.45 hrs THE EDER DAM

Buoyed by Shannon's apparent success, Henry Maudslay now tried again. But this time things didn't go as planned, in fact they went horribly wrong as AJ-Z released their Upkeep too late. The repercussions, as Wallis had predicted, were catastrophic as the great spinning mine struck the stone parapet with such velocity that it detonated on contact, the vivid explosion lighting up the entire valley.

Z-Zebra had passed over the spot only seconds before and was last seen banking violently before vanishing from view. Grantham, however, did receive their transmission – GONER 2 8 B – the mine has overshot the Eder with no damage apparent.

Those watching believed that the violent blast had done for Z-Zebra, but it hadn't. Only later was it discovered that at 02.36hrs Maudslay's aircraft had been shot down by flak as they approached the Dutch border on their way home, killing all the crew.

Back at the Eder the dam still stood and, after trying once again to contact the missing Astell, Gibson now knew that only one mine remained. It was slung under Les Knight's aircraft AJ-N.

BREACHING THE EDER DAM by Robert Taylor

Pilot Les Knight and his Flight Engineer Ray Grayston battle with the controls of Lancaster AJ-N in order to clear the hills immediately beyond the dam as their bomb explodes behind them, successfully breaching the Eder Dam.

N-NUTS
01.52 hrs THE EDER DAM

This would be the last throw of the dice for the First Wave. Far away to the east the sky was beginning to lighten; time and weapons had run out. Gibson told Les Knight to begin what would have to be the last attack.

Success, or otherwise, now depended on Knight and the crew of N-Nuts. Knight too had great difficulty approaching the dam but, on his second attempt, he struck lucky and at 01.52hrs managed a perfect release of his mine. It bounced three times and hit the dam wall almost in the centre. Now, as Knight pulled hard on the control column, his Flight Engineer Ray Grayston pushed the throttles forward and N-Nuts entered a steep banking climb to avoid the hill looming up fast ahead. In the front blister Bomb-Aimer Edward Johnson gritted his teeth and willed the aircraft to climb but back in the rear turret Canadian Harry O'Brien watched in awe as a column of water rose behind them as the massive explosion punched a vast hole through the dam's wall.

The message quickly flashed back to 5 Group – DINGHY – the second of Germany's mighty dams had been breached. They'd done it and, with all mines gone, there were no more targets for the First Wave. Gibson, Young, Shannon and Knight all turned for home.

For one of those crews, however, the story wasn't over as luck deserted Dinghy Young and the crew of A-Apple. They had come so far together, done so much and were nearly safe when, with only the North Sea ahead, they were hit by a flak battery on the Dutch coast. Lancaster AJ-A crashed in the flooding sands and, as with Maudslay's crew, there were no survivors.

...in the rear turret Canadian Harry O'Brien watched in awe as a column of water rose behind them as the massive explosion punched a vast hole through the dam's wall.

Original drawing by Richard Taylor

DAMBUSTERS by Anthony Saunders

After hitting the Eder Dam with pinpoint precision, Pilot Les Knight and Flight Engineer
Ray Grayston battle with the controls of Lancaster AJ-N in order to clear the hills
immediately beyond the dam as a torrent of water erupts behind them.

Original drawing by Richard Taylor

THE SECOND WAVE
INTO THE ABYSS

As Gibson arrived at the Möhne dam he was unaware of the disasters that fate had already thrown at the five aircraft in Second Wave heading for the Sorpe dam. Unlike the First Wave who flew in loose formation, the Second Wave were flying as singles and taking the longer northern route. Each aircraft had been scheduled to cross the Dutch coast over Vlieland, the second in the chain of low-lying islands covered by sand dunes and forests that stretch along the entire coastline of northern Holland, Germany and on to Denmark. Here they were to alter course and fly south-east, crossing the Zuider Zee before reaching their ultimate destination, the Sorpe.

E-EASY
23.50 hrs HALDERN, Nr EMMERICH on the Dutch / German border

Australian Bob Barlow in AJ-E, call sign Easy, had been the first to depart Scampton and had already made it to the German border when, at 23.50hrs, he flew into a pylon carrying high-tension cables, possibly after being hit by flak, and crashed just outside the village of Haldern. The chance of flying into such obstacles was one of the greatest risks associated with low-flying at night and everyone on the operation was only too well aware of it. Only luck had prevented several others from encountering the same fate.

LES MUNRO
by Richard Taylor

New Zealander and Captain of AJ-W, Les Munro was one of the three Flight Commanders on Operation Chastise.

Bob Barlow and his entire crew perished at the scene but, amidst the burning embers of AJ-E, the self-destruct mechanism on their Upkeep failed to detonate. It wasn't long before German bomb-disposal experts were on the scene and managed to defuse it. Vital knowledge of Barnes Wallis's secret weapon was now in enemy hands.

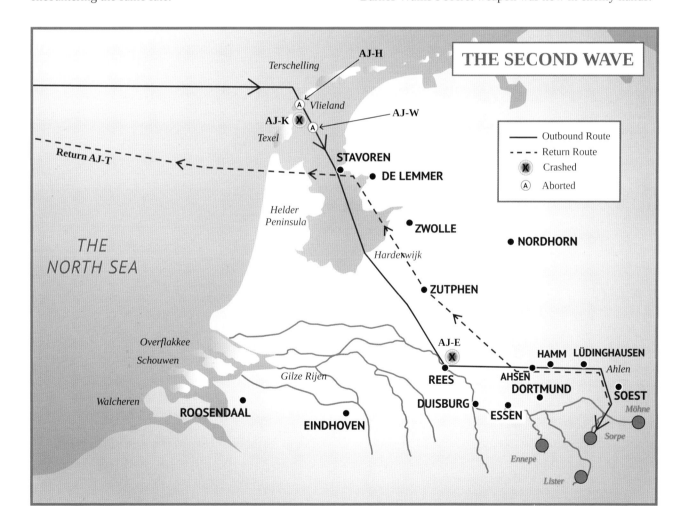

THE SECOND WAVE

Terschelling
AJ-H
Vlieland
AJ-K
Texel
AJ-W
Return AJ-T
STAVOREN
DE LEMMER
Helder Peninsula
Harderwijk
ZWOLLE
NORDHORN
THE NORTH SEA
ZUTPHEN
Overflakkee
Schouwen
Gilze Rijen
AJ-E
HAMM LÜDINGHAUSEN
Ahlen
AHSEN
REES
DORTMUND
Walcheren
DUISBURG
SOEST
ROOSENDAAL
ESSEN
Möhne
EINDHOVEN
Sorpe
Ennepe
Lister

— Outbound Route
--- Return Route
Ⓧ Crashed
Ⓐ Aborted

W-WILLIE
22.57 hrs OVER THE ISLAND OF VLIELAND

The tragic loss of Barlow and E-Easy, however, wasn't the first of the Second Waves troubles, nor would it be the last: Les Munro, the steadfast and reliable New Zealander who captained AJ-W, and who had been the second up behind Barlow, had unexpectedly encountered light flak over Vlieland shortly before 23.00hrs. Although no-one was wounded the damage to W-Willie was severe, especially to the wireless functions. The internal intercom was out, the VHF used to communicate with other aircraft was out, and the compass was destroyed. They couldn't talk to the outside world or to each other, save by writing notes and shouting word of mouth. Without the intercom especially, the task ahead would be impossible; pilot, bomb-aimer and flight engineer could never respond to instructions in time. Bitterly disappointed at the turn of events Les Munro had no choice but to abort, and at 23.06hrs with his mine still aboard, reluctantly turned for home.

H-HARRY by Richard Taylor

K-KING
22.57 hrs OFF TEXEL

Third up had been a Canadian, Pilot Officer Vernon Byers in AJ-K. But after take-off K-King was never heard from again. Like Munro and the others it was intended that they cross the Dutch coast at Vlieland but AJ-K had either strayed slightly south or, in the moonlight and at low-level, simply mistaken the islands' outlines and had flown over the heavily defended Texel instead. At 22.57hrs AJ-K was hit by flak and crashed into the sea just south of the island, killing everyone on board.

It was first loss of the night for Operation Chastise.

H-HARRY
23.06 hrs ZUIDER ZEE

Fourth up from Scampton in the Second Wave had been Flying Officer Geoff Rice at the controls of AJ-H. He had taken off at 21.31hrs and followed the assigned course perfectly until, just after crossing Vlieland, the perils of low-level flying claimed another victim. Rice had flown so low that he'd already nearly hit a sand dune on the island and shortly after H-Harry struck the water below, the force of the impact ripping the bomb off and filling the rear fuselage with seawater. Sergeant Stephen Burns, the rear gunner, was partially engulfed and only quick thinking, a quick reaction and incredible skills from Rice enabled H-Harry to climb clear. They'd all had a lucky escape but had lost their bomb. Their part in Operation Chastise was over and at 23.06hrs they turned for home.

Original drawing by Anthony Saunders

T-TOMMY
22.01 hrs RAF SCAMPTON

Of the Second Wave only Joe McCarthy, the sole American, flying T-Tommy, remained and his night had begun with problems before he'd even got off the ground. Assigned AJ-Q for the operation one of Queenie's engines began to rapidly lose coolant as they warmed up ready for take-off. It was obvious that AJ-Q could not fly and McCarthy and his crew hastily disembarked, spilling open one of the parachutes in the mêlée, and rushed to the only spare aircraft – AJ-T – where McCarthy discovered an essential 'compass deviation card' was missing. There was yet another delay as the missing card was found and a replacement parachute bundled aboard. McCarthy eventually got in the air at 22.01hrs, over half an hour late.

Four low-flying Lancasters had already flown over and the flak gunners on Vlieland and Texel were fully alert by the time T-Tommy crossed the coast. But McCarthy flew as low to the deck as he dared, later reporting that he 'flew between two large dunes to provide cover from the flak'! In the event they escaped unscathed and headed on for the Sorpe. It was an eventful journey for both gunners engaging searchlights and flak gunners; in the rear Dave Rodger had had a one-on-one duel with a light flak gun whilst, up front, Ron Batson had squirted his twin Brownings at 'an innocent-looking locomotive' only to discover it was a highly-defended flak train!

Fortune was shining on them, T-Tommy escaped, the only scratch being a burst starboard tyre caused by a single cannon shell.

'Concentration was key and everyone was playing his part. Joe never took us above about 100 feet or below 200mph, with Bill (Radcliffe, the Flight Engineer) coaxing every last morsel of performance out of the Merlins to try to make up time.'
George 'Johnny' Johnson DFM

Shortly after midnight McCarthy and his crew reached their destination – the Sorpe dam. They were the only ones from the Second Wave to do so.

Original drawing by Richard Taylor

SO CLOSE AT THE SORPE

'In the totally clear moonlight, it was an incredible sight. What we couldn't understand was why nobody else was there......The answer seemed horribly obvious, but there was no time to dwell on it. We still had a job to do.'

George 'Johnny' Johnson DFM

T-TOMMY
00.46 hrs THE SORPE DAM

As McCarthy took them over the undefended earth dam it was obvious that the topography, as at the Eder, would require enormous skill from both the pilot and bomb-aimer if their Upkeep was to be dropped as planned. Wallis and the planners had decided that being an earth dam, unlike the Möhne and Eder, the bomb at the Sorpe should be dropped un-spun from a position flying along and adjacent to the dam rather than from head on.

Steep hills, however, rose on either side and to the west lay the village of Langscheid where to complicate matters a large church steeple stuck up like a sore thumb. If they were to have any chance then, as George Johnson wrote, "Joe was going to have to fly the Lanc like a fighter aircraft".

Coming in over the village, banking hard around the steeple and diving sharply towards the dam Joe McCarthy had precious little time to align T-Tommy before climbing away sharply to avoid crashing into the hills on the far side. It took nine aborted attempts before, on their tenth run, George Johnson was satisfied enough to release the mine. It was 00.46hrs when his 'Bomb Gone!' was met with a 'Thank Christ for that!' from the rear turret; Dave

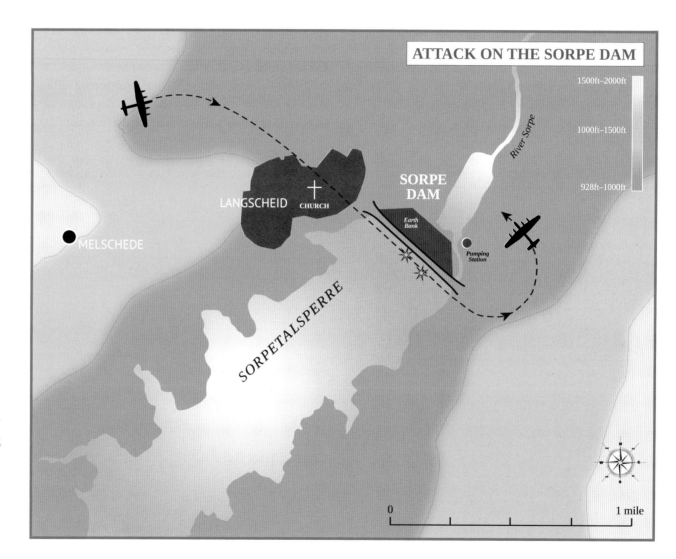

ATTACK ON THE SORPE DAM

MELSCHEDE

LANGSCHEID   CHURCH

SORPE DAM

Earth Bank

Pumping Station

River Sorpe

SORPETALSPERRE

1500ft–2000ft

1000ft–1500ft

928ft–1000ft

0   1 mile

◄ **ATTACKING THE SORPE** by Anthony Saunders

Joe McCarthy skilfully pilots AJ-T along the length of the Sorpe dam.

Rodger had just experienced the most uncomfortable roller-coaster ride of his life.

They had scored a direct hit but, once the tower of water had subsided, the dam was damaged along part of its crest but hadn't been breached. Disappointed not to have caused more damage but proud to have scored a bullseye, McCarthy and the crew of T-Tommy turned for home.

THE THIRD WAVE

Back at Scampton the five Lancasters that made up the Third Wave, the reserves, had been summoned into action, each detailed to attack one of the secondary targets. They were to follow the same outward route flown by Gibson's First Wave but, like those in the Second Wave, they were to fly as singles rather than any formation. Some of the misfortunes that had beset the Second Wave, however, were about to be repeated. Pilot Officer Bill Ottley was away first, departing Scampton just after midnight at the controls of C-Charlie.

C-CHARLIE
02.35 hrs Nr HAMM, Germany

At 02.30hrs, about half an hour after crossing the Dutch coast, C-Charlie was contacted by 5 Group and ordered to attack the Lister dam but within minutes of acknowledging they were coned by searchlights, hit by flak and set on fire. They had strayed a little too close to the heavily-defended city of Hamm, an important railway hub. The blazing aircraft crashed a few miles away killing all but one of Ottley's crew. Miraculously Sergeant

Freddie Tees the rear gunner survived badly-burned, to be taken prisoner. Trapped, his immobilised turret was blown clear as C-Charlie hit the ground and exploded.

S-SUGAR
02.00 hrs GILZE-RIJEN LUFTWAFFE AIRFIELD

Following Ottley off was Pilot Officer Lewis Burpee from the RCAF who took off from Scampton in AJ-S at 00.11hrs. They too strayed a little off course and either flew into flak near the Luftwaffe airfield at Gilze-Rijen, about 20 miles west of Eindhoven, or Burpee was simply dazzled by a searchlight beam. Whatever the cause, S-Sugar crashed on to the airfield buildings and exploded. There were no survivors.

F-FREDDIE
03.14 hrs THE SORPE DAM

Following the breaching of the Möhne dam Canadian Ken Brown and his all NCO crew were instructed to head for the Sorpe, the scene of Joe McCarthy's earlier attack. The third aircraft to depart in the final wave, they were up at 00.12hrs, a minute after Burpee. Brown crossed the Dutch coast only to find they were off course which necessitated some hasty recalculations during which Dudley Heal, the Navigator, discovered a 5% error in their compass. For the rest of the night he would have to allow for this in all his reckonings.

F-Freddie's journey was, like McCarthy's, also eventful and the two gunners soon found themselves busy shooting up some trains. Brown was also forced to take several violent manoeuvres along the way to avoid electricity pylons, trees and even a castle as they hedge-hopped over the countryside closing on the Sorpe, not helped by the mist that was steadily building in the valleys around. Their route took them over the shattered Möhne dam and all could see the massive breach and the water thundering through it.

The swirling fog that they'd been encountering along the way was in evidence at the Sorpe too, lying quite thickly across the water's surface. Nevertheless,

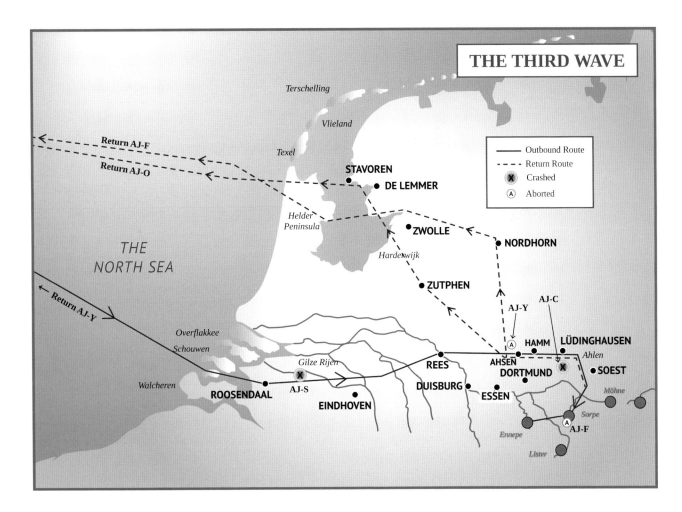

THE THIRD WAVE

Terschelling

Vlieland

Texel

THE NORTH SEA

Helder Peninsula

STAVOREN

DE LEMMER

Hardewijk

ZWOLLE

NORDHORN

ZUTPHEN

AJ-C

AJ-Y

Overflakkee

Schouwen

Gilze Rijen

REES

AHSEN

HAMM

LÜDINGHAUSEN

Ahlen

Walcheren

ROOSENDAAL

AJ-S

EINDHOVEN

DUISBURG

DORTMUND

ESSEN

SOEST

Möhne

Sorpe

AJ-F

Ennepe

Lister

Return AJ-F
Return AJ-O
Return AJ-Y

Outbound Route
Return Route
X Crashed
A Aborted

ATTACKING THE SORPE DAM by Richard Taylor

the hillsides were clear and Brown reckoned they could see well enough to attack but as Joe McCarthy had discovered earlier this was no piece of cake. All of Brown's great flying abilities would be needed and it took them almost as many attempts as George Johnson had

required until at 03.14hrs Steve Oancia, Brown's Bomb-Aimer, released the un-spun bomb. It too was bang on target on the water side of the dam and exploded with the by now familiar tower of water but, as they circled slowly in the moonlight, it was apparent that although further

damage had been caused, the dam had not been breached. Once again that night 5 Group received a GONER signal, this time followed by 7 8 C – Special weapon released, exploded on contact with the dam, no apparent breach, Target C (Sorpe). F-Freddie turned for home.

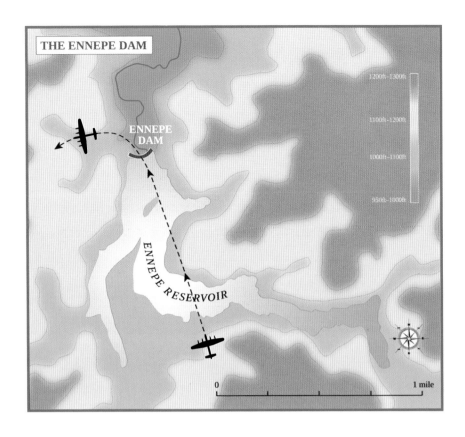

THE ENNEPE DAM

ENNEPE DAM

ENNEPE RESERVOIR

1200ft–1300ft

1100ft–1200ft

1000ft–1100ft

950ft–1000ft

0   1 mile

LAST STRIKE

THE ATTACK ON THE ENNEPE – OR WAS IT THE BEVER?

O f the nineteen aircraft that had set out from Scampton six had already perished by the time Bill Townsend in O-Orange reached the target he'd been detailed to attack, the Ennepe. Two more – Munro and Rice – had been forced to abort their mission and, apart from Brown at the Sorpe, only two Upkeeps remained intact, his and the one by Y-York.

O-ORANGE
03.37 hrs THE ENNEPE

Flying at tree-top level since crossing the Dutch coast at 01.31hrs, Pilot Officer Bill Townsend had had his work cut out avoiding the light flak batteries along the route. With the Möhne and Eder dams breached, 5 Group now diverted O-Orange to the Ennepe, but the heavy mist and fog that had now settled in many of the valleys made navigation along the new course a formidable challenge. With diligence and a degree of luck they eventually

found what they believed was the Ennepe but, as with McCarthy and Brown at the Sorpe, the surrounding hills and fog only added to the difficulties ahead.

At 03.37hrs, however, on their fourth attempt, Sgt Charles Franklin, the Bomb-Aimer, released the last Upkeep – it exploded as the others had done with a vast fountain of water. But Townsend's Upkeep had fallen short. George Chalmers, the Wireless Operator, tapped out 'GONER 5 8 E' to Grantham.

After the war it was discovered that, due to misidentification in the fog, Townsend had probably attacked the nearby Bever dam instead. Nevertheless, as Townsend turned O-Orange onto a course for home, they flew over the flood spewing out of the breached Möhne dam. After the inevitable encounter with searchlights and flak that plagued their journey home, O-Orange landed at 06.15hrs, the last aircraft to return from Operation Chastise.

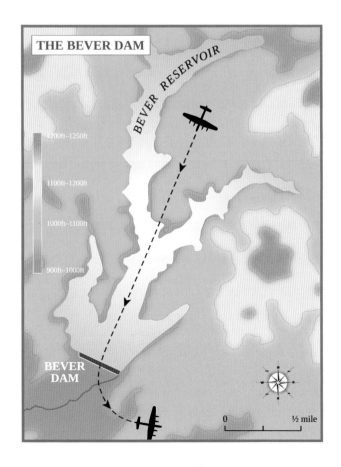

THE BEVER DAM

BEVER RESERVOIR

BEVER DAM

1200ft–1250ft

1100ft–1200ft

1000ft–1100ft

900ft–1000ft

0   ½ mile

Y-YORK
03.10 hrs north-east of HAMM

The last aircraft to leave Scampton on Operation Chastise, Flight Sergeant Cyril Anderson's all NCO crew in Y-York lifted off at 00.15hrs but, they too, were to endure a night of bad luck, mishap and disappointment. As with most of the other crews heavy flak had been a problem, but a malfunction of the rear guns meant they were hampered in dealing with a succession of searchlights encountered along the way. Avoiding both flak and searchlights contrived to throw Y-York off course several times and, as time went by, navigation was becoming a serious problem: the fog that earlier crews had reported building was getting worse, making the task

of identifying landmarks almost impossible. Directed to attack the Diemel dam, at 02.28hrs the problems facing Anderson increased with the receipt of orders diverting them to attack the Sorpe.

The Sorpe, however, was still a long way off. With dawn approaching, by the time they got to the dam – if they managed to find it in the fog – the sky would have lightened considerably, meaning that enemy flak would have a field day on the return journey. And, with his rear guns out, they would be easy pickings for enemy fighters. Reluctantly, therefore, at 03.10hrs, Anderson consulted his crew before deciding to abort the mission.

He touched down back at Scampton at 05.30hrs and, like Munro before him, landed with his mine still aboard.

Many would have turned back earlier, and for less pressing reasons but, ignoring any explanation, Gibson posted Anderson and his NCO crew off the squadron shortly after. There was no doubting their bravery, however, and a few months later the entire crew died in action together, shot down over Germany by an enemy night-fighter.

With the touch-down of O-Orange 45 minutes later Operation Chastise was over. It had been a success. After the congratulations, however, came the reckoning.

AFTERMATH

TUESDAY 18 May 1943

'DEVASTATION SWEEPS DOWN RUHR VALLEY' headlined the Daily Telegraph, continuing 'with one single blow the RAF has precipitated what may prove to be the greatest industrial disaster yet inflicted on Germany in this war.'

As readers digested the news, the 'devastating' floods had already carried everything before them: bridges, buildings, trees, vehicles and pylons; anything and everything swept into the broiling maelstrom that had scoured the valleys, mimicking in hours what natural erosion would have taken a thousand years to achieve.

By now 54 towns and villages had been inundated by 134 million tons of water and silt, mixed with raw sewage from ruptured pipes and facilities. A sea of sludge flowed unchecked through homes, factories and farms where fields would remain unusable for years. Waterworks and power stations had been destroyed, hundreds of electricity lines cut and railway lines swept away, track beds washed into oblivion and wagons tossed around like children's toys.

Sadly many prisoners of war, mainly Russians, were amongst the dead, drowned in the dark when their camp was engulfed by the 35ft high black wall of water that struck out of the night.

The great dams would never be the same again, at least for the duration of the war. Thousands of troops who would have been better employed on the Eastern Front, or later in Normandy, were brought in to defend them together with 70,000 forced labourers from the Organisation Todt, diverted away from building the Atlantic Wall. Although partially rebuilt, the Möhne and Eder lakes were thereafter kept at artificially low levels for fear of another raid.

In Britain and around the free world Operation Chastise was one of the great morale boosters of the war. For 617 Squadron, however, it was merely the beginning.

FOR VALOUR

"On conclusion of his third operational tour" announced the Supplement to The London Gazette on 25 May 1943, *"Wing Commander Gibson pressed strongly to be allowed to remain on operations and he was selected to command a squadron then forming for special tasks. Under his inspiring leadership, this squadron has now executed one of the most devastating attacks of the war – the breaching of the Möhne and Eder dams."*

"The KING has been graciously pleased to confer the VICTORIA CROSS on the undermentioned officer in recognition of most conspicuous bravery:-

Acting Wing Commander Guy Penrose Gibson DSO DFC (39438), reserve of Air Force Officers, No. 617 Squadron."

THE AWARDS

At 14.20hrs on 21 June 1943 a train pulled out of Lincoln station heading for London's Kings Cross via Grantham. Travelling in specially reserved carriages were many of the surviving members of 617 Squadron and the following day most of them were going to be decorated at Buckingham Palace for their part in Operation Chastise.

VICTORIA CROSS
Awarded for valour in the face of the enemy: A / Wg Cdr Guy Gibson DSO* DFC*

DISTINGUISHED SERVICE ORDER
Awarded for highly successful command and leadership during active operations:

Flt Lt Joe McCarthy DFC *(Captain AJ-T)*
Flt Lt David Maltby DFC *(Captain AJ-J)*
A / Flt Lt Harold Martin DFC *(Captain AJ-P)*
A / Flt Lt David Shannon DFC *(Captain AJ-L)*
Plt Off Les Knight *(Captain AJ-N)*

CONSPICUOUS GALLANTRY MEDAL (FLYING)
Awarded to non-commissioned ranks in recognition for acts of conspicuous gallantry in action against the enemy in the air:

F/S Ken Brown *(Captain AJ-F)*
F/S William Townsend *(Captain AJ-O)*

DISTINGUISHED FLYING CROSS
Awarded for exemplary gallantry during active operations against the enemy in the air:

Bar to the Distinguished Flying Cross
A / Flt Lt Robert Hay DFC *(Bomb Aimer AJ-P)*
A / Flt Lt Robert Hutchison DFC *(W/Op AJ-G)*
A / Flt Lt Jack Leggo DFC *(Navigator AJ-P)*
Fg Off Daniel Walker DFC *(Navigator AJ-L)*

Distinguished Flying Cross
A / Flt Lt Richard Trevor-Roper DFM *(Rear Gunner AJ-G)*
Fg Off Jack Buckley *(Rear Gunner AJ-L)*
Fg Off Leonard Chambers *(W/Op AJ-P)*
Fg Off Harold Hobday *(Navigator AJ-N)*
Fg Off Edward Johnson *(Bomb Aimer AJ-N)*
Plt Off George Deering *(Front Gunner AJ-G)*
Plt Off John Fort *(Bomb Aimer AJ-J)*
Plt Off Lance Howard *(Navigator AJ-O)*
Plt Off Frederick Spafford DFM *(Bomb Aimer AJ-G)*
Plt Off Torger Taerum *(Navigator AJ-G)*

DISTINGUISHED FLYING MEDAL
Awarded to non-commissioned ranks for an act or acts of valour, courage or devotion to duty whilst flying in active operations against the enemy:

Bar To the Distinguished Flying Medal
Sgt Charles Franklin DFM *(Bomb Aimer AJ-O)*

Distinguished Flying Medal
F/S George Chalmers *(W/Op AJ-O)*
F/S Don MacLean *(Navigator AJ-T)*
F/S Thomas Simpson *(Rear Gunner AJ-P)*
F/S Len Sumpter *(Bomb Aimer AJ-L)*
Sgt Dudley Heal *(Navigator AJ-F)*
Sgt George Johnson *(Bomb Aimer AJ-T)*
Sgt Vivian Nicolson *(Navigator AJ-J)*
Sgt Stefan Oancia *(Bomb Aimer AJ-F)*
Sgt John Pulford *(Flight Engineer AJ-G)*
Sgt Douglas Webb *(Front Gunner AJ-O)*
Sgt Raymond Wilkinson *(Rear Gunner AJ-O)*

Source: Supplement to The London Gazette of Tuesday 25 May 1943

CREW LIST – OPERATION CHASTISE

'We had done what was asked of us, we had done it to the best of our ability, and we were all still alive. It didn't do to dwell on thoughts of the faces missing from the mess.'
Squadron Leader George 'Johnny' Johnson

Of the 133 airmen who set out from RAF Scampton on Operation Chastise only 77 returned. Of the 56 who didn't make it back, only 3 survived, a terrible loss rate. Among the dead were the two flight commanders – S/Ldrs Maudslay and Young, and Hopgood, Gibson's deputy for the Möhne dam attack.

THE FIRST WAVE

AJ G LANCASTER ED932

Pilot & Captain:	Wg Cdr **GUY GIBSON** DSO* DFC*
Flt/Engineer:	Sgt **JOHN PULFORD**
Navigator:	P/O **TORGER TAERUM**
W/Op:	Flt Lt **BOB HUTCHISON** DFC
Bomb Aimer:	P/O **FREDERICK SPAFFORD** DFM
Front Gunner:	F/Sgt **GEORGE DEERING**
Rear Gunner:	Flt Lt **RICHARD TREVOR-ROPER** DFM

Up at 21.39 hrs   Landed at 04.15 hrs
First a/c to attack the Möhne dam.

AJ M LANCASTER ED925
Failed to return

Pilot & Captain:	Flt Lt **JOHN HOPGOOD** DFC*
Flt/Engineer:	Sgt **CHARLES BRENNAN**
Navigator:	F/O **KENNETH EARNSHAW**
W/Op:	Sgt **JOHN MINCHIN**
Bomb Aimer:	F/Sgt **JIM FRASER**
Front Gunner:	P/O **GEORGE GREGORY** DFM
Rear Gunner:	P/O **ANTHONY BURCHER** DFM

Up at 21.39 hrs   Crashed at 00.34 hrs 3 miles from the dam
Second a/c to attack the Möhne dam, damaged by flak on approach and by the detonation of his overshot Upkeep. The Bomb Aimer and Rear Gunner survived to become PoWs.

AJ P LANCASTER ED909

Pilot & Captain:	Flt Lt **HAROLD MARTIN** DFC
Flt/Engineer:	P/O **IVAN WHITTAKER**
Navigator:	Flt Lt **JACK LEGGO** DFC
W/Op:	F/O **LEONARD CHAMBERS**
Bomb Aimer:	Flt Lt **BOB HAY** DFC
Front Gunner:	P/O **TOBY FOXLEE** DFM
Rear Gunner:	Flt Sgt **THOMAS SIMPSON**

Up at 21.39 hrs   Landed at 03.19 hrs
Third a/c to attack the Möhne dam.

AJ A LANCASTER ED877
Failed to return

Pilot & Captain:	S/Ldr **MELVIN YOUNG** DFC*
Flt/Engineer:	Sgt **DAVID HORSFALL**
Navigator:	F/Sgt **CHARLES ROBERTS**
W/Op:	Sgt **LAWRENCE NICHOLS**
Bomb Aimer:	F/O **VINCENT MacCAUSLAND**
Front Gunner:	Sgt **GORDON YEO**
Rear Gunner:	Sgt **WILFRED IBBOTSON**

Up at 21.47 hrs   Crashed at 02.58 hrs
Fourth a/c to attack the Möhne dam causing the beginning of a breach. Shot down by flak over the Dutch coast. There were no survivors.

AJ J LANCASTER ED906

Pilot & Captain:	Flt Lt **DAVID MALTBY** DFC
Flt/Engineer:	Sgt **WILLIAM HATTON**
Navigator:	Sgt **VIVIAN NICHOLSON**
W/Op:	Sgt **ANTHONY STONE**
Bomb Aimer:	P/O **JOHN FORT**
Front Gunner:	Sgt **VICTOR HILL**
Rear Gunner:	Sgt **HAROLD SIMMONDS**

Up at 21.47 hrs   Landed at 03.11 hrs
Last a/c to attack the Möhne dam, Upkeep on target causing major breach.

AJ L LANCASTER ED929

Pilot & Captain:	Flt Lt **DAVID SHANNON** DFC
Flt/Engineer:	Sgt **ROBERT HENDERSON**
Navigator:	F/O **DANIEL WALKER** DFC
W/Op:	F/O **BRIAN GOODALE** DFC
Bomb Aimer:	Flt Sgt **LEN SUMPTER**
Front Gunner:	Sgt **BRIAN JAGGER**
Rear Gunner:	F/O **JACK BUCKLEY**

Up at 21.47 hrs   Landed at 04.08 hrs
First a/c to attack the Eder dam.

AJ Z LANCASTER ED937
Failed to return

Pilot & Captain:	S/Ldr **HENRY MAUDSLAY** DFC
Flt/Engineer:	Sgt **JOHN MARRIOTT** DFM
Navigator:	F/O **ROBERT URQUHART** DFC
W/Op:	W/O **ALDEN COTTAM**
Bomb Aimer:	P/O **MICHAEL FULLER**
Front Gunner:	F/O **WILLIAM TYTHERLEIGH** DFC
Rear Gunner:	Sgt **NORMAN BURROWS**

Up at 21.59 hrs   Crashed at 02.36 hrs
Damaged by explosion from his Upkeep at the Eder and then hit by flak on return flight over Netterden nr Emmerich, Germany. There were no survivors.

AJ B LANCASTER ED864
Failed to return

Pilot & Captain:	Flt Lt **BILL ASTELL** DFC
Flt/Engineer:	Sgt **JOHN KINNEAR**
Navigator:	P/O **FLOYD WILE**
W/Op:	W/O **ABRAM GARSHOWITZ**
Bomb Aimer:	F/O **DONALD HOPKINSON**
Front Gunner:	F/Sgt **FRANCIS GARBAS**
Rear Gunner:	Sgt **RICHARD BOLITHO**

Up at 21.59 hrs   Crashed at 00.15 hrs
Flew into high-tension cables and pylon near Marbeck on outward flight. There were no survivors.

AJ N LANCASTER ED912

Pilot & Captain:	P/O **LES KNIGHT**
Flt/Engineer:	Sgt **RAY GRAYSTON**
Navigator:	F/O **HAROLD HOBDAY**
W/Op:	F/Sgt **BOB KELLOW**
Bomb Aimer:	F/O **EDWARD JOHNSON**
Front Gunner:	Sgt **FREDERICK SUTHERLAND**
Rear Gunner:	Sgt **HARRY O'BRIEN**

Up at 21.59 hrs   Landed at 04.20 hrs
Third a/c to attack the Eder causing breach.

THE SECOND WAVE

AJ E LANCASTER ED927
Failed to return

Pilot & Captain:	Flt Lt **ROBERT BARLOW** DFC
Flt/Engineer:	P/O **SAMUEL WHILLIS**
Navigator:	F/O **PHILIP BURGESS**
W/Op:	F/O **CHARLES WILLIAMS** DFC
Bomb Aimer:	P/O **ALAN GILLESPIE** DFM
Front Gunner:	F/O **HARVEY GLINZ**
Rear Gunner:	Sgt **JACK LIDDELL**

Up at 21.28 hrs   Crashed at 23.50 hrs
Flew into high-tension cables on outward leg at Haldern, Germany. There were no survivors.

AJ W LANCASTER ED921

Pilot & Captain:	Flt Lt **LES MUNRO**
Flt/Engineer:	Sgt **FRANK APPLEBY**
Navigator:	F/O **GRANT RUMBLES**
W/Op:	W/O **PERCY PIGEON**
Bomb Aimer:	Sgt **JAMES CLAY**
Front Gunner:	Sgt **WILLIAM HOWARTH**
Rear Gunner:	Flt Sgt **HARVEY WEEKS**

Up at 21.29 hrs   Landed at 00.36 hrs
Damaged by flak on outward leg. Mission aborted.

THE MORNING AFTER by Gerald Coulson

A single Lancaster, one of the lucky ones to have made it safely back to base, stands proudly alone as if in tribute to those who didn't return.

AJ●K LANCASTER ED934
Failed to return

Pilot & Captain:	P/O **VERNON BYERS**
Flt/Engineer:	Sgt **ALISTAIR TAYLOR**
Navigator:	F/O **JAMES WARNER**
W/Op:	Sgt **JOHN WILKINSON**
Bomb Aimer:	P/O **ARTHUR WHITTAKER**
Front Gunner:	Sgt **CHARLES JARVIE**
Rear Gunner:	F/Sgt **JAMES McDOWELL**
Up at 21.30 hrs	Crashed at time unknown

Hit by flak on outward leg over Texel. There were no survivors.

AJ●H LANCASTER ED936

Pilot & Captain:	P/O **GEOFFREY RICE**
Flt/Engineer:	Sgt **EDWARD SMITH**
Navigator:	F/O **RICHARD MacFARLANE**
W/Op:	W/O **CHESTER GOWRIE**
Bomb Aimer:	W/O **JOHN THRASHER**
Front Gunner:	Sgt **THOMAS MAYNARD**
Rear Gunner:	Sgt **STEPHEN BURNS**
Up at 21.31 hrs	Landed at 00.47 hrs

Hit the sea on outward leg ripping away his Upkeep. Mission aborted.

AJ●T LANCASTER ED825

Pilot & Captain:	Flt Lt **JOE McCARTHY** DFC
Flt/Engineer:	Sgt **WILLIAM RADCLIFFE**
Navigator:	F/Sgt **DON MacLEAN**
W/Op:	F/Sgt **LEONARD EATON**
Bomb Aimer:	Sgt **GEORGE JOHNSON**
Front Gunner:	Sgt **RONALD BATSON**
Rear Gunner:	F/O **DAVE RODGER**
Up at 22.01 hrs	Landed at 03.23 hrs

First a/c to attack the Sorpe dam.

THE THIRD WAVE

AJ●C LANCASTER ED910
Failed to return

Pilot & Captain:	P/O **WARNER OTTLEY** DFC
Flt/Engineer:	Sgt **RONALD MARSDEN**
Navigator:	F/O **JACK BARRETT** DFC
W/Op:	Sgt **JACK GUTERMAN** DFM
Bomb Aimer:	Flt Sgt **THOMAS JOHNSTON**
Front Gunner:	Sgt **HARRY STRANGE**
Rear Gunner:	Sgt **FREDDIE TEES**
Up at 00.09 hrs	Crashed at 02.35 hrs

Hit by flak on the outward leg nr Hamm. Only the Rear Gunner survived and became PoW.

AJ●S LANCASTER ED865
Failed to return

Pilot & Captain:	P/O **LEWIS BURPEE** DFM
Flt/Engineer:	Sgt **GUY PEGLER**
Navigator:	Sgt **THOMAS JAYE**
W/Op:	P/O **LEONARD WELLER**
Bomb Aimer:	F/Sgt **JAMES ARTHUR**
Front Gunner:	Sgt **WILLIAM LONG**
Rear Gunner:	W/O **JOSEPH BRADY**
Up at 00.11 hrs	Crashed at 02.00 hrs

Hit by flak on the outward leg nr Gilze-Rijen airfield in Holland. There were no survivors.

AJ●F LANCASTER ED918

Pilot & Captain:	F/Sgt **KEN BROWN**
Flt/Engineer:	Sgt **BASIL FENERON**
Navigator:	Sgt **DUDLEY HEAL**
W/Op:	Sgt **HARRY HEWSTONE**
Bomb Aimer:	Sgt **STEVE OANCIA**
Front Gunner:	Sgt **DANIEL ALLATSON**
Rear Gunner:	F/Sgt **GRANT MacDONALD**
Up at 00.12 hrs	Landed at 05.33 hrs

Second a/c to attack the Sorpe dam.

AJ●O LANCASTER ED886

Pilot & Captain:	F/Sgt **BILL TOWNSEND** DFM
Flt/Engineer:	Sgt **DENNIS POWELL**
Navigator:	P/O **LANCE HOWARD**
W/Op:	F/Sgt **GEORGE CHALMERS**
Bomb Aimer:	Sgt **CHARLES FRANKLIN** DFM
Front Gunner:	Sgt **DOUGLAS WEBB**
Rear Gunner:	Sgt **RAYMOND WILKINSON**
Up at 00.14 hrs	Landed at 06.15 hrs

Only a/c to attack the Ennepe dam.

AJ●Y LANCASTER ED924

Pilot & Captain:	F/Sgt **CYRIL ANDERSON**
Flt/Engineer:	Sgt **ROBERT PATTERSON**
Navigator:	Sgt **JOHN NUGENT**
W/Op:	Sgt **WILLIAM BICKLE**
Bomb Aimer:	Sgt **JOHN GREEN**
Front Gunner:	Sgt **ERIC EWAN**
Rear Gunner:	Sgt **ARTHUR BUCK**
Up at 00.15 hrs	Landed at 05.30 hrs

Experienced navigational problems and a turret malfunction. Mission aborted.

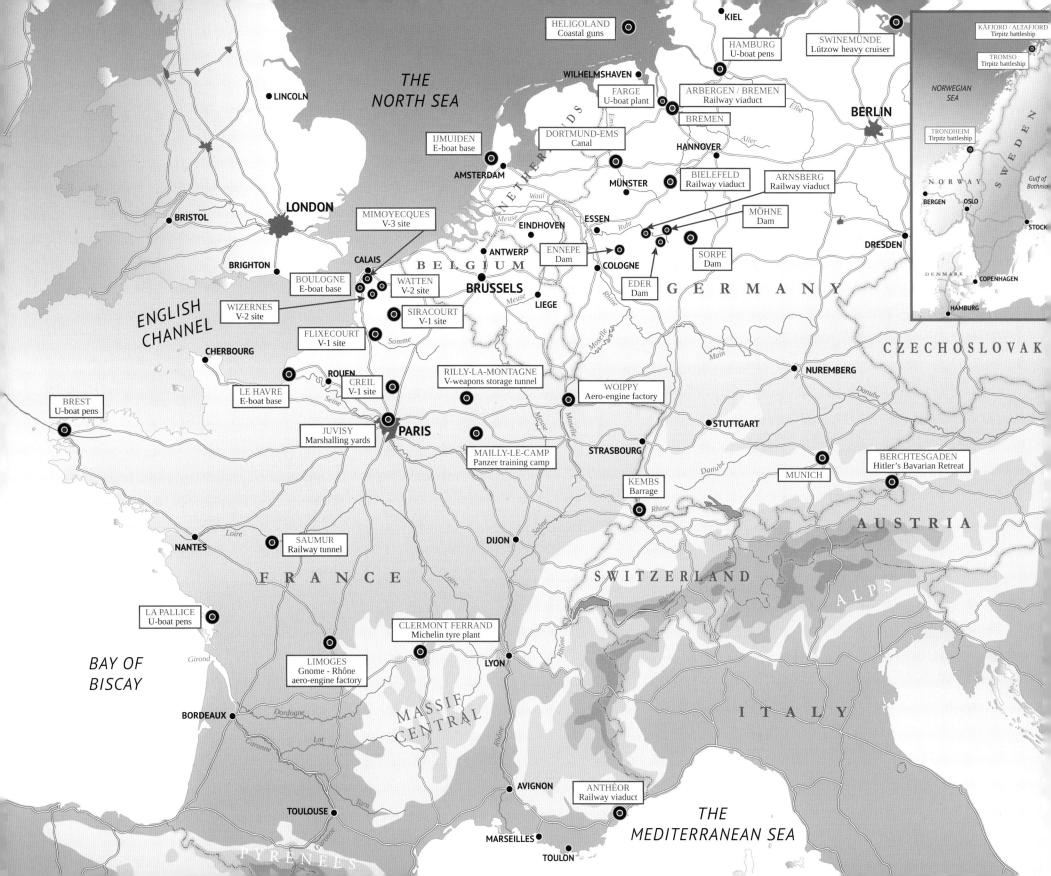

KIEL

HELIGOLAND
Coastal guns

HAMBURG
U-boat pens

SWINEMÜNDE
Lützow heavy cruiser

THE
NORTH SEA

WILHELMSHAVEN

LINCOLN

FARGE
U-boat plant

ARBERGEN / BREMEN
Railway viaduct

BERLIN

BREMEN

DORTMUND-EMS
Canal

HANNOVER

IJMUIDEN
E-boat base

AMSTERDAM

LONDON

MÜNSTER

BIELEFELD
Railway viaduct

ARNSBERG
Railway viaduct

BRISTOL

MIMOYECQUES
V-3 site

MÖHNE
Dam

EINDHOVEN

ESSEN

BRIGHTON

ANTWERP

ENNEPE
Dam

SORPE
Dam

CALAIS

BELGIUM

BRUSSELS

COLOGNE

DRESDEN

BOULOGNE
E-boat base

WATTEN
V-2 site

LIEGE

EDER
Dam

GERMANY

ENGLISH
CHANNEL

WIZERNES
V-2 site

SIRACOURT
V-1 site

CHERBOURG

FLIXECOURT
V-1 site

Somme

CZECHOSLOVAK

ROUEN

RILLY-LA-MONTAGNE
V-weapons storage tunnel

WOIPPY
Aero-engine factory

NUREMBERG

LE HAVRE
E-boat base

CREIL
V-1 site

Seine

BREST
U-boat pens

JUVISY
Marshalling yards

PARIS

STUTTGART

MAILLY-LE-CAMP
Panzer training camp

STRASBOURG

Danube

KEMBS
Barrage

MUNICH

BERCHTESGADEN
Hitler's Bavarian Retreat

Rhine

Danube

NANTES

SAUMUR
Railway tunnel

Loire

SWITZERLAND

AUSTRIA

ALPS

LA PALLICE
U-boat pens

CLERMONT FERRAND
Michelin tyre plant

LYON

BAY OF
BISCAY

Girond

LIMOGES
Gnome - Rhône
aero-engine factory

Rhône

ITALY

BORDEAUX

Dordogne

Lot

MASSIF
CENTRAL

Garonne

Garonne

AVIGNON

ANTHÉOR
Railway viaduct

TOULOUSE

THE
MEDITERRANEAN SEA

Tarn

PYRENEES

MARSEILLES

TOULON

KÅFJORD / ALTAFJORD
Tirpitz battleship

NORWEGIAN
SEA

TROMSO
Tirpitz battleship

TRONDHEIM
Tirpitz battleship

NORWAY

BERGEN

OSLO

Gulf of
Bothnia

SWEDEN

STOCK

DENMARK

COPENHAGEN

HAMBURG

PART THREE
A RETURN TO OPERATIONS

'It was now all over and peace reigned at Scampton. The hangars were silent and the Lancasters moored at their dispersal points were waiting for the next job of work. The Ruhr squelched in the mud caused by the operation against the Möhne and Eder dams, while all over Britain the men who had helped to execute this major disaster, as far as the Germans were concerned, were taking a few days' well-earned rest.'

Flight Lieutenant Harry Humphries, Adjutant of 617 Squadron from its formation until a few weeks before the end of the war.

The 'few days' rest', however, turned into a month of inactivity whilst Bomber Command tried to decide what to do with their new squadron of low-flying experts. The respite, however, was unsettling for all concerned and after a while the tag 'one-op squadron' was no longer amusing – it began to rankle.

Whilst several replacement crews arrived and Squadron Leader George Holden was posted in to replace Guy Gibson as Commander, the squadron re-equipped with standard Lancasters. Those in charge of Bomber Command were also making the decision to keep the squadron together and operational in the role for which it had been formed – a specialist precision-bombing unit which, from September onwards, would have a new squadron code with KC replacing AJ.

After several weeks of doing little except a never-ending stream of training flights, on 15 July a moderately successful raid was carried out against the switching station at San Polo d'Enza in northern Italy; a trip that involved flying on to Algeria to land, re-fuel and re-arm. On their return trip to Scampton the squadron bombed the docks in the Italian port of Livorno. The only other activities were so-called 'Nickel' raids – leaflet drops – again flown over Italy, and to much grumbling amongst the crews. They wanted more action.

At the end of August the squadron moved the 20 or so miles south-east to RAF Coningsby which, with its newly-installed concrete runways, was far more suitable for heavy bomber operations than the grass field at Scampton. Within days of their arrival, however, the 'buzz' went around the messes that once again the squadron had been selected for another 'special' operation.

If the action everyone was hoping for was welcomed, their chosen target wasn't. It was the Dortmund-Ems canal, already one of the biggest thorns in Bomber Command's side.

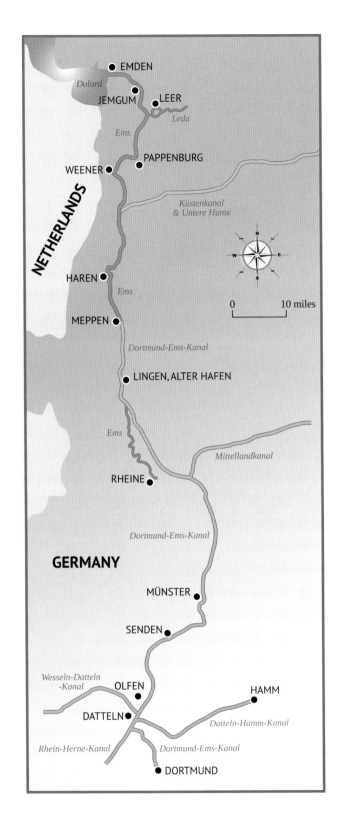

DISASTER STRIKES
ATTACK ON THE DORTMUND-EMS CANAL

'Perhaps it was as well that the crews were ignorant of their next task. It would not be pleasant to know that one had only a few weeks to live. The single difference between the life of an average bomber crew and a condemned man was that the bomber boys didn't know the date.'

Flight Lieutenant Harry Humphries, Adjutant of 617 Squadron

Completed in 1899 and opened by no less a person than the Kaiser himself, the Dortmund-Ems canal had become one of the most important canals in Europe. Linking Dortmund, and the heavy industries of the Ruhr, to the North Sea almost 170 miles away, the Dortmund-Ems was in part a series of inter-connecting canals linked by locks and lifts which flows north into the canalised River Ems.

Much of the traffic south was Swedish ore destined for the coal fields of Westphalia, whilst coal and steel flowed north. But well before the outbreak of war much of that steel was in the shape of tanks, guns, munitions and Hitler's other essential weapons of war.

Strategic points along the canal had been heavily attacked by the RAF before, and quickly repaired by the Germans. Now, on the night of 14 / 15 September 1943 in its first operation from Coningsby, it was 617 Squadron's turn.

THE NORTH SEA off Cromer

The raid got off to a bad start: carrying 12,000lb high-capacity 'cookies' for the first time and led by their new Commanding Officer, a force of eight Lancasters departed for the target – aqueducts on the Dortmund-Ems near Ladbergen – when bad weather en-route led to their recall. The raid had been aborted. All would have been well but somewhere off Cromer Squadron Leader David Maltby crashed into the sea for reasons unknown. The man who had finally breached the Möhne dam breach was dead, along with all his crew.

THE DORTMUND-EMS CANAL
15 / 16 September 1943

The following night things got worse when in what has been described as 'the blackest day in history of 617 Squadron', the same crews attempted to repeat the low-level operation with Mick Martin replacing Maltby.

'I was awarded a bar to my DFC for a raid on the Dortmund-Ems canal when only 3 aircraft (one of which returned early), out of a force of 8 returned home (5 aircraft being lost). I had spent 40 minutes at low-level in the target area in poor visibility being continually under fire from light flak while searching for the right place to drop my 12,000lb cookie.'
Squadron Leader Dave Shannon DSO DFC

Dortmund-Ems Canal

The raid on the Münster Aqueducts 12 / 13 August 1940.

With the German invasion of Belgium and France in 1940 following the so-called 'Phoney War' the Dortmund-Ems became an obvious, but difficult target. Between June and September 1940, Hampdens from several squadrons had made a score of daring but costly attacks at various strategic points along its length, none more so than the raid on the night of 12 / 13 August. A force of five Hampdens, drawn from 49 and 83 Squadrons, was selected to attack the twin Münster aqueducts, supposedly one of the canal's more vulnerable parts. Having watched all four preceding aircraft be hit, Flight Lieutenant Roderick 'Babe' Learoyd made his attack. The citation for the Victoria Cross that he was about to win – the first VC to be awarded in Bomber Command during World War II – described what happened next:

"...was well aware of the risks entailed. To achieve success it was necessary to approach from a direction well known to the enemy, through a lane of especially disposed anti-aircraft defences, and in the face of the most intense point-blank fire from guns of all calibres. The reception of the preceding aircraft might well have deterred the stoutest heart, all being hit and two lost. Flight Lieutenant Learoyd nevertheless made his attack at 150 feet, his aircraft being repeatedly hit and large pieces of the main plane torn away. He was almost blinded by the glare of many searchlights at close range, but pressed home this attack with the greatest resolution and skill. He subsequently brought his wrecked aircraft home...'

Three years later it would be 617's turn to run the gauntlet.

Still hampered by bad weather and with fog obscuring the target, the flak both en-route and around the canal was brutally intense. The raid was a disaster: George Holden, the new Commanding Officer, was shot down before reaching the target, his crew included four who had flown on Operation Chastise with Gibson. Another dams veteran, Pilot Officer Les Knight who had breached the Eder, died too; the perils of low-level flying at last catching up with him when he hit a stand of trees. With his aircraft badly damaged and losing the power to climb he struggled at the controls to gain enough height for his crew to bail out. All did so, except Knight, who died as the stricken bomber crashed.

Three other aircraft were brought down by the flak; they included the Lancasters of Flt Lt Wilson and P/O Divall, both of whom were scheduled to fly on Operation Chastise but, owing to sickness amongst their crews, didn't take part. Their reprieve was brief.

Only David Shannon and Mick Martin came near to hitting the target; neither caused much damage. The low-level raid had been a disaster, five out of eight aircraft – each carrying a crew of eight that included an extra gunner – had been lost, along with 33 lives. The squadron had been decimated. Instead of 'the one-op' tag and new one was coined – 'the suicide squadron.'

LEONARD CHESHIRE
by Richard Taylor

'He was in many ways the opposite of Guy Gibson. No less courageous or tactically astute, his personal character meant he endeared himself to the squadron personnel immediately. He was friendly and approachable; taking time to talk to all ranks... He was, quite simply, the best commander I ever served under.'
Squadron Leader George 'Johnny' Johnson DFM

CHESHIRE TAKES COMMAND

Following the death of George Holden, Mick Martin had been promoted to assume temporary command but, apart from a successful trip to attack the Antheor Viaduct in southern France, the squadron did little more than slowly rebuild.

But, on 10 November 1943, Leonard Cheshire arrived to take over command.

Highly decorated and already a famous name within the RAF, Cheshire had willingly taken a drop in rank to command 617 Squadron and the chance to fly again. Charming, sociable and considerate, Cheshire was the sort of man who talked to everyone regardless of their rank – the very opposite of Gibson. His looks were quite different, too: the Australian author Paul Brickhill, who had been a Spitfire pilot with 92 Squadron and later

THE STRAGGLER RETURNS by Robert Taylor

a prisoner of war, wrote after the war that 'whereas Gibson had looked the part; Gibson and glamour were indivisible, Cheshire looked more like a theological student thinly disguised as a Senior Officer; yet he had done two tours and won a DSO and bar, and a DFC. He was tall, thin and dark, a strange blend of brilliance (sometimes erratic), self-conscious, confidence and soft-spoken charm.'

They might not have undertaken many raids but, as with the weeks before Operation Chastise, Martin's squadron had been training hard but this time their work had little to do with the ultra low-level flying they'd all been used to. In fact it was the very opposite.

Ever since the start of the war Bomber Command had struggled to find ways of improving accuracy and reducing losses. Hitting targets from 20,000ft was difficult enough in perfect daylight but almost impossible at night; all too often bombs were scattered across too wide an area to cause maximum damage. And losses amongst the bomber crews remained depressingly high as on average one bomber in 25 failed to return. The chance of surviving a full tour of 30 operations was low.

One solution had come from Don Bennett, the creator and inspiration of his specialist Pathfinder Force, whose sole job was to find the target and mark it with coloured flares, giving the main bomber force a point at which to aim. The Pathfinders had improved the accuracy of mass-bombing considerably but precision bombing from high altitude, especially with one of the new 10-ton bombs Barnes Wallis was perfecting, remained a challenge until the arrival of SABS – the Stabilised

for the job, ordering Martin and his 617 crews to practice ultra-accurate high-level bombing practice 'till your eyes drop out. You've got to get down to an average of under a hundred yards from 20,000ft!'

The challenge was immense: to hit the bullseye would mean releasing their bomb two miles before the target and calculating the rate of descent over the 45 seconds the bomb took to fall. Such was the calibre of 617 Squadron that by the time Cheshire arrived their accuracy was down to an error margin of just 90yds.

On the night of 16 / 17 December 1944 Cheshire led nine Lancasters from his new squadron on a raid for the first time. Their target was a V-1 construction site in

to do things his way and contrary to orders, dived his Lancaster down to 400 feet and placed his marker on the nail. This time both the marker and target were obliterated.

Cheshire was impressed. Like many others he considered Martin the greatest bomber pilot of the war and later wrote 'I learned all that I know of this low-flying game from Mick. He showed me what

DAY DUTIES FOR THE NIGHT WORKERS
by Robert Taylor

Automatic Bomb Sight which included a gyro. SABS, however, had one serious drawback: to work it needed a long, straight and unwavering ten mile run-in. Enemy flak would have a field day. A large, conventional bomber force would be decimated.

AVM Cochrane at 5 Group, however, thought that if a small, highly-trained unit could hit the target with one of the new monster bombs there would be no need to send in a larger force. He chose his squadron of experts

woods near Flixecourt, about 20 miles south of Abbeville. Unfortunately the high-level marker dropped by a Mosquito from the Pathfinders fell short of the target by some 350 yards, but such was 617 Squadron's accuracy that not one of their 12,000lb bombs fell more than 100 yards from the markers. The target survived.

It was some weeks later, on 22 January 1944, when they attacked another V-1 site in the Pas-de-Calais that Martin, frustrated by the events at Flixecourt, decided

you could do by coming in straight and hard and low, and I never saw him make a mistake.' On the night of 8 / 9 February 1944 Cheshire had the opportunity to put Martin's low-level diving technique to the test for himself. This time the target this time was the Gnome et Rhône aero engine factory at Limoges. Gnome et Rhône had produced aero engines since the First World War and, after the German invasion of France, was forced to manufacture BMW 801 radial engines for the Fw190.

A LINCOLNSHIRE SUNSET by Gerald Coulson

As the sun sets over their Lincolnshire airfield, the men of 617 Squadron prepare their aircraft for another mission.

The destruction of the plant would seriously hinder production.

Wanting to inflict maximum destruction but minimum loss of French civilian life Cheshire, skilfully avoiding a pair of water towers and a tall factory chimney, made three low-level passes over the factory to warn the 500 workers to escape (all did so bar one who returned for his bicycle) and waiting five minutes before he, then Martin, dropped their marker flares from just 50 feet. Such was the accuracy that all but one of the squadron's bombs landed inside the factory compound and the factory was obliterated.

Four days later, however, Martin's influential spell with 617 Squadron came to an end when, on another attack on the Antheor viaduct, his aircraft was hit by flak, killing Bob Hay the bomb-aimer and badly wounding Whittaker, the flight engineer. It was all Martin could do to fly the stricken Lancaster on its two remaining engines to the safety of Sardinia. The crew had been together since 1941 and had vowed to 'take the hint' if anyone was killed and come off ops. All but Martin who, nevertheless, felt he had to leave the squadron. "It seemed an unbelievable decision" wrote 617's adjutant Flight Lieutenant Harry Humphries, "but he meant it. The funny thing was that he left us to become a night-fighter pilot, for a rest he said. Some fellows have a peculiar idea of rest!'

The New Year of 1944 had seen 617 Squadron transfer to RAF Woodhall Spa, one of Coningsby's former satellites. It would remain their home for the rest of the war.

MUNICH
24 April 1944

The attack on the Gnome et Rhône factory was typical of Cheshire's concern for inflicting as few civilian casualties as possible. On 15 / 16 March, for instance, the precision of their attack on the Michelin tyre plant in Clermont Ferrand had resulted in the factory being destroyed but the nearby workers' canteen remained intact.

Success of their low-level marking techniques on precision raids in France had led some in command to scepticism about its suitability for use on mass raids into the heart of Germany. On the night of 24 / 25 April Cheshire and 617 Squadron set off before a force of 260 Main Force bombers to attack Munich. In place of Martin, Dave Shannon was now flying as Cheshire's deputy. Over the target the flak was intense – as were the searchlights – but Cheshire dropped his markers right on target and Shannon dropped his on top of Cheshire's, intensifying the target for the main force.

Shannon recalled being coned in searchlights as he climbed away 'with flak exploding all around. It was an exciting 10 minutes before I managed to shake them off and ask my navigator, Len Sumpter, for a course for base. Len's laconic reply – "when I get my night vision back perhaps I'll find my maps, meantime for God's sake fly west!" They made it back as far as Manston, touching down at dawn with 'about 5 minutes' fuel to spare.'

SUPERCOOKIE by Richard Taylor

617 Ground crew load a massive 12,000lb 'Supercookie' blast bomb at RAF Consingsby, September 1943.

LANCASTER by Robert Taylor ▶

Flt Lt Bill Reid VC in his Lancaster KC-S during Operation Taxable in the early hours of D-Day, 6 June 1944.

OPERATION TAXABLE
THE ART OF DECEPTION

617 SQUADRON BRIEFING ROOM
02 May 1944

At the beginning of May the squadron were once again to be taken off operations to embark on a month of solid training. Although surprised by the tight security as they traipsed into the briefing room, few had any idea of the momentous news they were about to hear from the senior officer standing in front of them – AVM the Hon Ralph Cochrane, Commander of 5 Group.

Cochrane began by simply announcing: 'Gentlemen, the next time you are airborne it will be D-Day!'

After the cheers had died down he went on to say that the long-awaited invasion of Europe was to happen in a few weeks' time and stressed the need for the utmost secrecy. 617 Squadron, he said, were to play a vital part: it would be their job to participate in one of the most elaborate acts of electronic deception of the war. Their job was to help persuade the Germans that the invasion was about to begin, but not in Normandy. Operating in

conjunction with a flotilla of small launches and pinnaces under the code-name *Taxable*, they were going to create a large 'ghost' armada heading slowly towards the French coast near Cap-d'Antifer, just south of Fécamp and over sixty miles to the east of *Sword* beach.

To confuse any of the German coastal radar units that had survived the bombing during the build up to D-Day, complex plans had been devised and drawn up by the TRE – Telecommunications Research Establishment – a little known but vital group of scientists based at Malvern in rural Worcestershire. They had devised a way of imitating the progress of a huge slow-moving convoy through the creation of a continuous radar echo that covered an area of approximately 250 square miles, the rough size of a potential invasion fleet. For the plan to work, however, would require precision flying and exceptional navigational skills, and for the next few weeks 617 Squadron trained as hard and relentlessly as they'd ever done.

Just before midnight on the night of 5 / 6 June 1944 that training was over and the invasion was on. Leonard Cheshire led the first two waves of eight Lancasters away from Woodhall Spa and headed south.

THE ENGLISH CHANNEL
5 / 6 June 1944

The intense night-time navigational skills and flying capabilities required of Cheshire's eight Lancaster crews would have to be as good as they'd been on Operation Chastise, perhaps better. Each aircraft was carrying at least 12 men, a far bigger crew than normal which included a co-pilot, an extra navigator, radar and radio operators, and men fore and aft to dispatch their cargo of 'window' or 'chaff' – bundles of thin aluminium strips – through chutes fore and aft.

The first wave of four aircraft was to fly long, elliptical orbits in a two-mile wide line abreast. Each aircraft would fly at 3,000 feet and at a constant speed of

OPERATION GLIMMER: *Whilst 'Taxable' was in progress 218 Squadron, flying Stirlings, carried out a similar operation to simulate an invasion convoy heading for Boulogne and the Pas-de-Calais.*

OPERATION TITANIC: *Designed to suggest other airborne landings away from the main drop zones, a force of 40 Halifaxes, Hudsons and Stirlings dropped units of 'Ruperts' – dummy parachutists made from sand and straw stuffed into human-shaped canvas bags that exploded and caught fire on landing*

OPERATION MANDREL: *Operating out of their bas in Norfolk, 16 Stirlings of 199 Squadron used 'Mandrel' – a radar jamming system – to create an electronic screen behind which the real invasion fleet hid from German radar. They were joined by B-17s from the USAAFs 803rd Bomb Squadron.*

OPERATION 'A B C': *Operating between 'Taxable' and 'Glimmer' was a force of 21 Lancasters from 101 Squadron, a specialised countermeasures unit equipped with 'Airborne Cigar' or 'A B C' – a system designed to jam Luftwaffe radio contact between ground controllers and any night-fighters who might be prowling amongst the Allied airborne landings.*

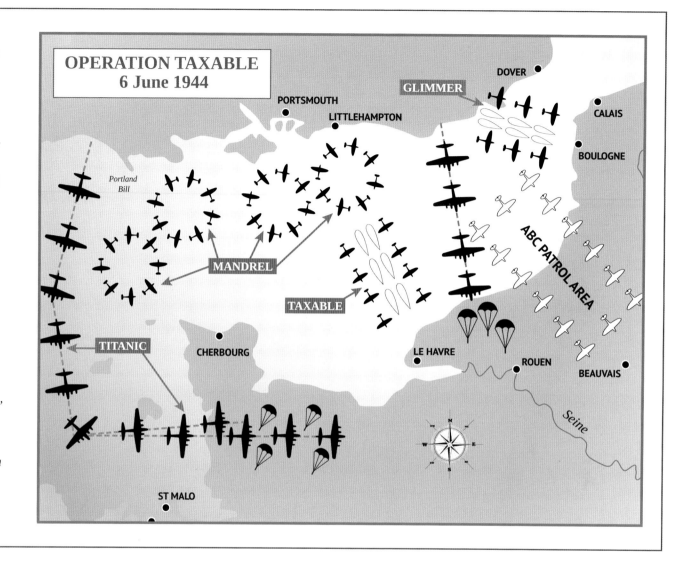

OPERATION TAXABLE
6 June 1944

180mph whilst the extra 'bods' dispatched their bundles of 'chaff' at the rate of exactly 12 bundles per minute, one every three seconds.

Eight miles behind the first wave the second wave repeated the same operation and at the southern end of their ellipse the aircraft would slowly turn 180 degrees, advancing one mile out to sea with each orbit.

As the cloud of 'chaff' fell beneath the Lancasters it was designed to reflect any enemy radar looking seawards, with the aim of creating the illusion of an 'invasion' fleet. At the same time a flotilla of small launches headed towards France at 8 knots, towing large radar-reflecting 'moonshine' balloons to help in the 'ghost fleet' deception and, whilst towing their balloons, the little ships kept up a flow of radio signals between the non-existent fleet.

After two hours flying, as the 'chaff' ran out, the remaining eight aircraft in the third and fourth waves slipped seamlessly into place. As the Germans puzzled over the fleet's direction, far to the west the airborne landings had already happened and shortly the first landing craft in the real invasion fleet were about to hit *Utah* beach. Their job done, it was time for 617 Squadron to go home.

'Our job done, we headed home for breakfast and, possibly, sleep. We felt very sorry indeed for the poor blighters we passed in their troop transports and gliders, heading the other way, many on a one-way ticket.'
Bill Reid VC, 617 Squadron.

RETURN TO WOODHALL SPA by Richard Taylor

Lancaster KC-W, flown by Sqn Ldr Les Munro and co-pilot Wg Cdr Leonard Cheshire, returns
to RAF Woodhall at the conclusion of Operation Taxable, 6 June 1944.

FOR VALOUR
BILL REID VC

Flt Lt Bill Reid was one of three Victoria Cross pilots to have flown with 617 Squadron. Joining the squadron in January 1944 shortly after he had been awarded the VC, he flew with them until the end of the war. Bill Reid earned the country's highest award for bravery after an event that happened on the night of 3 / 4 November 1943 whilst he was serving with 61 Squadron:

BILL REID VC
by Richard Taylor

'We were detailed to attack Düsseldorf. My windscreen was shattered by a Me110 just after crossing the Dutch coast, and I was hit in the head, shoulders and hands, As soon as the Me110 had been driven off, an Fw190 attacked. This time we were strafed from stem to stern.

My navigator was killed, my wireless operator fatally injured, the flight engineer and I were both also hit. With most systems out of commission I had to use my memory to fly on to the target, and the moon and Pole Star to return to England.

We later discovered that we had been bang on target, though this did not make up for my sadly missed crew members.

I was flying the usual operations over Germany and reacted like most raw recruits in being rather tense until we had our target instructions. Beyond this point one had so much to do that there was no time to think of the dangers ahead. This fact, in my opinion, bears out my claim regarding my feelings on the night of 3 November that year. I chose not to turn back when we were shot up by the German fighters because we would have been flying against the wave of other Allied bombers. One makes what seems the right operational decision at the time and it does not seem 'heroic' as this incident was later described.

After this raid I spent 5 weeks in hospital and a further 3 weeks on sick leave. I was then told by AVM Cochrane that I was to join 617 Squadron at Woodhall Spa, where I reported on 13 January 1944.'

On 31 July Bill Reid's luck ran out when, bombing a V-weapon storage site at Rilly-la-Montagne east of Paris from 16,000ft, his aircraft was hit by a stick of bombs as another Lancaster from the main bomber stream mistimed its bomb run.

Only Reid and his wireless operator managed to exit the doomed aircraft as it broke up in the air and plunged vertically into the ground, killing the rest of his crew. Both were taken prisoner.

NO TURNING BACK by Robert Taylor

During the mission on which he was awarded the Victoria Cross, Flt Lt Bill Reid's 61 Squadron Lancaster comes under attack from an Fw190 night-fighter en-route to Düsseldorf, 3 / 4 November 1943.

THE RAID ON THE SAUMUR TUNNEL
by Richard Taylor

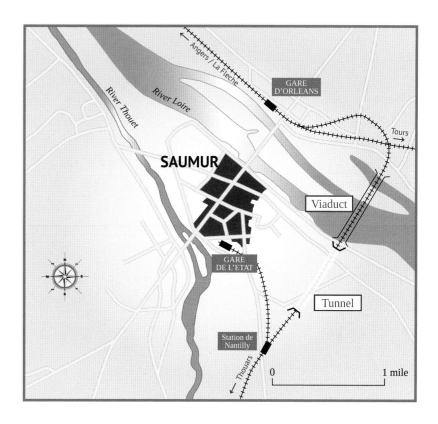

THE TUNNEL AND THE TALLBOY

THOUARS, north of Poitiers
8 June 1944

A few days after Operation Taxable, 617 Squadron was once again called upon to make another important contribution to the success of the on-going invasion. As thousands of Allied troops continued to pour ashore, the Germans increasingly came to realise that Normandy, not the Pas-de-Calais, was the real place of invasion and swiftly recovering from their initial doubts, now attempted to rush reinforcements to the front.

One of those units was the 17.SS-Panzergrenadier-Division *Götz von Berlichingen* based at Thouars, just north of Poitiers, about 250 miles away in western

France. The Division consisted of six full infantry battalions, most of which were motorised, along with 42 Sturmgeschütz IV assault guns. If the Germans could move them north quickly enough then their input might prove decisive as the Allied beachhead enlarged and pushed deeper inland. Reports received from the French Resistance suggested that the panzergrenadiers were already packed and ready to move. They must be stopped, and quickly.

The obvious way to do that was to cut the rail link that ran north from Poitiers but railway track can be quickly repaired. Something much more long-lasting was needed and the planners swiftly chose the best place of

all – the railway tunnel on the south side of Saumur. If the tunnel was closed off it would take the Germans several days to divert the panzergrenadiers through other links.

Saumur was an ancient town on the River Loire. Overlooked by a beautiful château and surrounded by some of the most famous vineyards in France it was also a vital rail hub linking Normandy to the south. If they wanted to get north in a hurry, 17.SS-Panzergrenadier-Division *Götz von Berlichingen* had no choice but to go via Saumur.

With the target quickly selected it was now up to 617 Squadron to destroy it. And this time, as with their attack on the dams a year earlier, they were going to use another of Barnes Wallis's new inventions for the first time – a massive 12,000lb 'earthquake' bomb named 'Tallboy'.

Wallis had been working on his idea for a ground-penetrating 'earthquake' bomb for some time and, unlike existing blast bombs which exploded on the surface, Wallis had designed his new 12,000lb Tallboys to penetrate the earth alongside large structures and drill deep underground before the warhead – containing 5,200lbs of *Torpex*, the explosive used in Upkeep and 50% more powerful than TNT – detonated. Each had a 25-second delay fuse. The resulting explosion would trigger a mini-earthquake whose seismic shockwaves would destroy anything above and around, leaving a vast crater over 100ft wide and 80ft deep.

Each Tallboy was virtually hand-built, many parts finely engineered from hardened steel and laboriously assembled. Such was their cost that the Air Ministry considered them too valuable to be jettisoned in the case of an aborted sortie so, whatever the risk to themselves, crews were ordered to bring any unused bombs home.

By June 1944 the Tallboy was ready for use and the tunnel at Saumur would be on the receiving end.

BOMBING UP
by Richard Taylor

PIERCED BY A TALLBOY
by Richard Taylor

The inside of the Saumur railway tunnel
following the detonation of one of Tallboys
on the night of 8 / 9 June 1944.

SAUMUR
02.08 hrs 8 / 9 June 1944

Most, but not all, of the 25 Lancasters that left Woodhall Spa carried a Tallboy, the new bomb was still in short supply but when, at 02.08hrs Cheshire gave the order to bomb, the results were breathtaking. Whilst one Mosquito was to mark the northern end of the tunnel close to the bridge over the Loire, Cheshire, in another Mosquito, marked the southern portal. Diving to 500 feet he placed the red marker flares with his customary expertise, close to the tunnel entrance and watched with satisfaction as Tallboy after Tallboy exploded deep underground, half of them hitting within 100yds of the markers.

The area was cratered like the moon with one bomb detonating inside the tunnel, opening the tunnel to the sky. Similar strikes were hitting the northern end: those aircraft not carrying Tallboys straddled and hit the bridge with 1,000lb bombs.

The operation was a great success: the tunnel had been destroyed and was impassable. It was never fully repaired until long after the war was over but, more importantly, the progress north of the 17.SS-Panzergrenadier-Division *Götz von Berlichingen* was badly disrupted. The delay of diversion cost them dearly and it would be several more days before they reached Normandy and got into action.

V-1 LAUNCH
by Richard Taylor

HITLER'S REPRISAL WEAPONS

BETHNAL GREEN
04.30 hrs 13 June 1944

Exactly a week after D-Day, the first V-1 fell on London. At 04.15hrs on the morning of 13 June a member with the Royal Observer Corps spotted a 'bright, yellow glow in the dark' in the sky over Kent; they were the flickering flames from the engine propelling a pilotless, cigar-shaped flying-bomb heading towards London. As the fuel ran out the bomb fell, its 2,000lb warhead exploding near the ancient A2 Watling Street,

just outside Swanscombe, a small town south of the Thames. Minutes later another V-1 landed on a railway bridge in London's Bethnal Green, killing six people. Catapulted from ramps in northern France the V-1s' reign of terror, in which over 6,000 civilians would be killed and thousands more injured, had begun.

The V-weapon attacks, however, had been expected. The existence of Hitler's *Vergeltungswaffen* – reprisal weapons – had been known about for some time; in August the previous year Bomber Command had sent a

force of over 600 aircraft to attack the known V-weapon testing site and research facility at Peenemunde on Germany's far northern Baltic coast.

There was believed to be another weapon, apart from the V-1. Whilst the V-1 was, more or less, a conventional bomb with wings, its big brother was in a different league altogether. Brainchild of Wernher von Braun, Germany's brilliant rocket scientist who confessed to having dreams of sending men to the moon, his V-2 was nothing less than a quantum step forward in rocket technology – a

Original drawing by Robert Taylor

state-of-the-art ballistic missile capable of 3,500mph and, once in flight, unstoppable.

617 Squadron and others had long been playing their part in trying to destroy and disrupt the construction of V-weapon assembly and launch sites before the weapons could be used. The very first raid on which Cheshire had led the squadron, back in December 1943, had been against a construction site near Flixecourt, 20 miles south of Abbeville. Others followed as Bomber Command and the USAAF began a systematic attack, but now that a V-1 had finally been launched in anger, the pace of the raids increased.

A series of massive reinforced concrete bunkers with tunnels stretching deep underground formed the heart of the V-weapon operations in the Pas-de-Calais. The V-1 assembly bunker at Siracourt was rendered unusable by massive air raids and the site at Lottinghem, where construction started later, was abandoned almost at once. But to eradicate the huge, reinforced concrete facilities built to house V-2s at Watten and Wizernes, and another facility at Mimoyecques would need all the help that 617 Squadron and its Tallboys could bring.

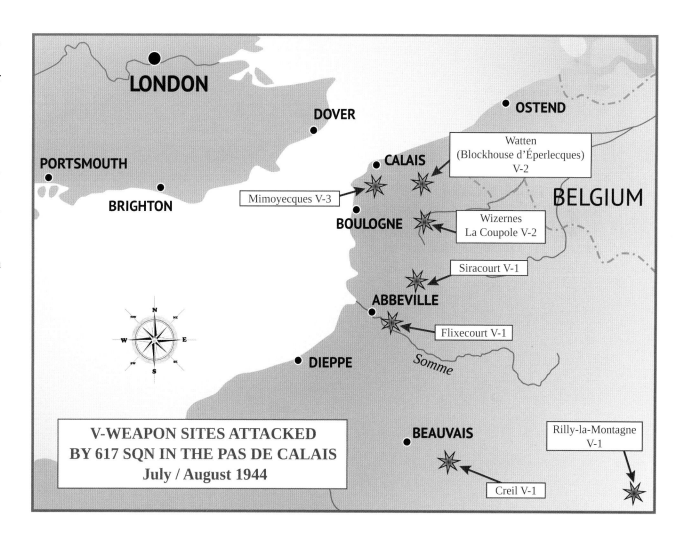

V-WEAPON SITES ATTACKED BY 617 SQN IN THE PAS DE CALAIS
July / August 1944

WATTEN
19 June 1944

'...the "Tallboys"...vanished in a wisp of dust in the moment of impact. They had eleven-second delayed fuses and the seconds dragged till the ground burst in the shadow of the concrete and tens of thousands of tons of earth reared up in a climbing mushroom'
Paul Brickhill (The Dam Busters)

BUNKER BUSTERS by Richard Taylor

Lancasters from 617 Squadron pound the V-1 storage bunker and launch site at
Siracourt in the Pas-de-Calais with 12,000lb Tallboys, 25 June 1944.

BLOCKHOUSE IN THE FORÊT ÉPERLECQUES, Nr Watten
19 June 1944

For over a year the Germans had been at work in the woods near Watten. Using an army of conscripts, prisoners of war and slave labour the huge construction site was impossible to fully conceal. At first its intended use puzzled the Allies who understood, however, that if the Germans were constructing something so big it must be important. For that reason alone, it must be destroyed. Many raids followed and it didn't take long for Military Intelligence to work out the site's real purpose – a V-2 launch site complete with facilities for producing the liquid oxygen propellant needed to fuel each rocket.

Whilst blast bombs from the previous heavy bombing had devastated the surrounding area, only 617 Squadron's Tallboy earthquake-bombs could have any chance of penetrating the blockhouse's 16ft thick reinforced concrete roof. Not that it had to. Wallis was confident that the deep, underground shock waves released by a Tallboy exploding nearby might prove equally effective in undermining the bunker and its foundations, perhaps even more so.

On 19 June, 17 Lancasters from 617 Squadron attacked the Éperlecques blockhouse with Tallboys followed by a raid a month later. Out of 32 Tallboys one penetrated alongside the target and Wallis was right: the whole structure was shaken so violently that any thought of keeping highly volatile and unstable liquid oxygen there could lead to oblivion. The site was abandoned before any V-2 assembly and production had even begun and the Germans transferred their efforts to the nearby site at Wizernes protected, or so they thought, by one of the largest, and probably the thickest, concrete domes ever built.

LA COUPOLE, WIZERNES
20 June 1944

About three miles south of St Omer stood a deep quarry from which, before the war, limestone had been hewn. In 1943 the Germans found another use for it, a V-2 assembly, storage and launch site constructed on a monumental scale. Underground galleries and vast subterranean chambers were linked by tunnels bored into the hillside from rocket-sized, five-feet thick blast doors in the side of the quarry and, above it all, shielding it from bombing attack, one of the largest concrete domes ever built – La Coupole.

As with the site near Watten, the area around the site had been turned into a bleak landscape of destruction by thousands of conventional bombs, but La Coupole was undamaged. Later, on 17 July, 617 Squadron flew to Wizernes with their Tallboys to finish it off. Although the dome remained intact three Tallboys exploded by the entrance, one detonated just under the dome and another exploded in one of the tunnels, the combined shock waves being enough to undermine the dome and collapse the hillside. The site was inoperable and abandoned. It was now no longer possible to launch V-2 rockets on the industrial scale the Germans had planned; all future launches would be restricted to small, mobile units operating from Belgium, Holland and finally from within Germany itself.

V-1 by Robert Taylor

After the war von Braun worked for the Americans and on 16 July 1969 watched as another of his rockets – Saturn V – lifted off from Cape Kennedy with the crew of Apollo 11. His dream of sending men to the moon had become reality.

MIMOYECQUES – V-3
6 July 1944

The bunker at Mimoyecques near Boulogne was also thought to be a rocket facility but it wasn't. Only when the abandoned site was overrun by advancing Canadian troops in September 1944 was its real purpose discovered – an underground battery containing five of an intended 25 gigantic, smooth-bore, super-guns aimed at London. Unknown to the Allies, had the third of Hitler's

Vergeltungswaffen – the V-3 – survived, 600 shells an hour might have rained down on Britain's capital.

On 6 July 1944, Leonard Cheshire led the daylight attack to destroy the site. Departing from Woodhall Spa at 14.25 in his newly-acquired Mustang he was over the target, still heavily defended by flak despite all the previous bombings, about an hour later. Ignoring it, Cheshire dived down to 800 feet and marked the bunker with red spotfires before calling his bombers in. As with

the attack at Wizernes it didn't matter if the Tallboys were spot on or just very close – the seismic shock from their underground detonations were enough to collapse the underground shafts, tunnels and chambers, entombing the operatives and several hundred slave workers. Mimoyecques was finished, the V-3 super-guns were finished and another of Hitler's dreams was over.

For Leonard Cheshire his time with 617 Squadron was also over. Having completed 100 operations and four full tours it was time to hand over command to someone else. He had rebuilt the squadron, endowed it with a new sense of purpose and everyone was sad to see him go. In September the London Gazette announced that Leonard Cheshire had become the second Commanding Officer of 617 Squadron to be awarded the Victoria Cross, unusually not for a single action but for '…four years of fighting against the bitterest opposition he has maintained a record of outstanding personal achievement, placing himself invariably in the forefront of the battle. What he did in the Munich operation was typical of the careful planning, brilliant execution and contempt for danger which has established Wing Commander Cheshire a reputation second to none in Bomber Command.'

At the same time as taking Cheshire off operations, AVM Cochrane stood down three of the original Operation Chastise pilots – Dave Shannon, Les Munro and Joe McCarthy. They had earned their rest and an era was over. It was time for someone else to take over the reins. His name was James Tait.

V-2 LAUNCH by Richard Taylor

Launched from mobile sites more than 1,400 V-2 rockets were fired against England.

SUMMER HARVEST by Gerald Coulson

In the midst of the harvest in the late summer of 1944, a 617 Squadron
Lancaster makes its final approach towards RAF Woodhall Spa.

'A thoughtful man with light brown eyes that look through and beyond one. A man of few words, but words that count.'

Andrew Boyle (No Passing Glory)

PART FOUR
JAMES 'TIRPITZ' TAIT
WORTHY SUCCESSOR

JAMES 'TIRPITZ' TAIT
by Richard Taylor

◀ **CLOUD COMPANIONS** by Robert Taylor

Stepping into the shoes of Gibson and Cheshire was a big task for anybody; both were hard acts to follow. But the man chosen for the job – Wing Commander James Tait – was equal to the task.

Known to his bomber crews as 'Willie', by the time he was posted to command 617 Squadron he was one of the most respected officers in Bomber Command and, with two DSOs and a DFC to his name, highly decorated.

In 1940, as a Flight Commander with 51 Squadron, he had flown Whitleys into Germany and taken part in the first raid on Italy, crossing the Alps in a terrifying thunderstorm. He had flown on the first raid to Berlin before taking command of the squadron, leading them to Malta to take part in Operation Colossus – an airborne assault on a viaduct in southern Italy and the first British Army parachute raid of the war.

He then commanded 35 Squadron, the first to be equipped with the new Halifax before being given temporary command of Don Bennett's 10 Squadron after Bennett had been shot down in one of the early attacks on the German battleship *Tirpitz*. Bennett narrowly evaded capture and made it back to England but, in his absence, Tait led 10 Squadron on the early 1000-bomber raids. On Bennett's return, in July 1942 Tait was given command of 78 Squadron, the sister squadron of 76 Squadron commanded by one Leonard Cheshire. Both men got on well and co-operated closely, and although officially constrained by the number of times they could fly operations, both led raids whenever they could.

After a spell at Headquarters, Willie Tait joined 5 Group as a Master Bomber and spent the night before D-Day controlling a force of 200 Lancasters over the Cherbourg peninsula eliminating coastal defences at Saint-Pierre-du-Mont. But the thing for which he is best remembered was still to come. James Tait would be the man who finally sunk the *Tirpitz*.

◄ THE BUNKER AT LA PALLICE
by Richard Taylor

With construction still in progress, one of the first U-boats
from the 3rd Flotilla is already using the huge new bunker
at La Pallice, western France, December 1941.

DIRECT HIT by Simon Smith

Flt Lt Tony Iveson releases his Tallboy to score a direct hit
on the Brest U-boat pens, 5 August 1944.

THE U-BOAT PERIL

WEST OF IRELAND
19.45 hrs 3 September 1939

On the day that Britain declared war on Germany,
torpedoes fired from the U-30 sank the liner SS
Athenia, en-route to Canada, with great loss of life.
She was the first British ship lost in World War II and
the continued threat posed by the U-boats, although
diminished by the Battle of the Atlantic, remained until
the last day of the war.

With the concrete bunkers of the V-weapon sites
put out of action and the Allied armies breaking out of
Normandy, 617 Squadron and their Tallboys increasingly
sought out some of the Reich's other hardened concrete
fortresses – the massive U-boat pens that had been
constructed along the French Atlantic coast such as
those at Brest, La Rochelle and Lorient, where German
garrisons were still holding out. There were more in

Norway and closer to home in Holland, Bremen and
Hamburg.

Protected seaward by massive floating blast doors,
each line of pens was capable of berthing entire U-boat
flotillas and protected overhead by reinforced concrete,
granite slabs and hardened steel roofs had defied all
attempts to penetrate them. Brest, the most westerly
harbour of all, had been attacked over 80 times without
success. Now it was 617's turn to attack using Tallboys.

THE HOMECOMING by Robert Taylor

Escorted by Fw190s from III./JG2, a small group
of U-boats from the Kriegsmarine's 9th U-boat
Flotilla return to their home port of Brest in 1942.

BREST HARBOUR
5 August 1944

Tait led the daylight raid and marked the target well.
The sight of the pens below him was spectacular, alive
with heavy flak; an area well over half a million square
feet covered by heavily-reinforced concrete. In places the
roof was 20ft thick.

This was the first of three raids over the next eight
days during which the squadron dropped a total of 26
Tallboys scoring nine direct hits, five of which penetrated
the bunker roof. The U-boat safe haven at Brest was no
longer safe and the last intact U-boat soon left, heading
for Norway. There was, however, one more target in Brest
harbour for 617 to deal with – the remains of the obsolete

French cruiser *Gueydon*. It was thought that the Germans were about to tow it and other hulks into the mouth of the port and sink them as a 'blockships'. On 13 August 1944, whilst some aircraft attacked the pens with Tallboys others, using their famed pinpoint precision, sank both the cruiser and a tanker with 1,000lb bombs before either could be moved.

Throughout the month of August the pens at the other ports received the same treatment as those at Brest. Brest finally fell to the Americans on 21 September 1944 after a month-long battle, one with a high cost – over 10,000 casualties. It was a figure the Allies were not going risk repeating in capturing La Rochelle, St Nazaire and Lorient. Now that the U-boat pens and harbours were out of commission and inoperable the Allies simply surrounded the ports and cordoned them off. They finally surrendered in May 1945.

LETTING THE LIGHT IN
by Richard Taylor

The vast circular hole left in the roof of a U-boat pen in Brest after a direct hit by a Tallboy.

THE ATTACK ON THE KEMBS BARRAGE
by Richard Taylor

Lancaster KC-W, flown by Sqn Ldr John Cockshott, attacks the
Kembs Barrage at 16.54hrs, 7 October 1944.

> *'It would have to be done very accurately; that meant doing it in full daylight, and the dam was circled with guns. The bombers would have to fly very low, straight and level, and run the gauntlet. No question as to who should do it!'*
> **Paul Brickhill (The Dam Busters)**

KEMBS BARRAGE
THE 'OTHER' DAMS RAID

KEMBS BARRAGE north of Basel
16.51 hrs 7 October 1944

The Möhne and Eder were not the only dams breached by 617 Squadron. There was another at Kembs, a great barrage stretching across the upper reaches of the Rhine to the south of Mulhouse. The barrage not only generated hydro-electricity but made the river navigable upstream towards Basel in Switzerland.

It was for neither reason, however, that the dam was attacked; it was because the advancing Allied armies were sweeping through France towards the Rhine. It was feared that if the Germans opened the flood gates, any army attempting to cross the river nearby would have a wall of water unleashed upon it. Not only would it stop the crossing but, more importantly, thousands would drown. Far better to pre-plan and smash the dam

now, giving the floodwaters ample time to subside and dissipate. There was only one unit up to the task – 617 Squadron.

This might have been a golden opportunity for them to repeat another Upkeep operation, but there wasn't time to adapt the Lancasters, prepare new mines, or to train. They were given a week. And the plan they came up with was as daring as any they'd ever attempted before.

On the afternoon of Saturday 7 October 1944, Willie Tait led a force of thirteen Lancaster s across France in company with Mustangs from 133 Wing, 2nd Tactical Air Force. The plan was simple but would require split-second timing. Eight aircraft, acting as decoys to distract the heavy flak, flew in at 8,000ft from the west. As soon as their bombs, with 25-second delayed-action fuses, exploded, the Mustangs caused further disruption

by diving on the enemy gun batteries whilst, at the same moment, Tait and the remaining six Lancasters sneaked in at low level from the opposite direction.

Leading from the front, Tait's aircraft was badly hit but he pressed on and at 16.51hrs dropped his Tallboy on target, just short of the sluice-gates. His bomb, fitted with a half-hour delayed-action fuse, struck the target. The others followed.

Although, sadly, two crews were lost to the intense flak, the raid was a great success. After 30 minutes Tait's Tallboy detonated and breached the flood-gates, releasing so much water barges upstream to Switzerland were stranded high and dry. When the French First Army eventually crossed the Rhine nearby, there was now one less obstruction in their way.

SINKING THE TIRPITZ

Churchill had once ordered the Admiralty to simply 'SINK THE BISMARCK'.
Now, in an equally terse memo he demanded 'WHERE IS TIRPITZ?'

Sister ship to the *Bismarck* and sharing its elegant lines, the 45,900 ton *Tirpitz* was the largest battleship in Hitler's Navy, and one of the most powerful warships in the world. The 'Pride of the Kriegsmarine' was sleek, fast yet heavily-armoured, and equipped with the latest

weaponry in a vast arsenal that included eight 15-inch guns. Should *Tirpitz* ever succeed in breaking out into the North Atlantic she would cause chaos, wreaking havoc amongst the Allied convoys with potentially catastrophic

results for the war. Churchill increasingly called her 'The Beast'.

From the moment her keel had been laid RAF Bomber Command had tried to destroy her – without much success – and, on the night of 14 / 15 January 1942, *Tirpitz* slipped quietly through the Kiel canal heading for the fjords of Norway. Thanks to the code-breakers at Bletchley it was soon discovered that the battleship was holed up near Trondheim.

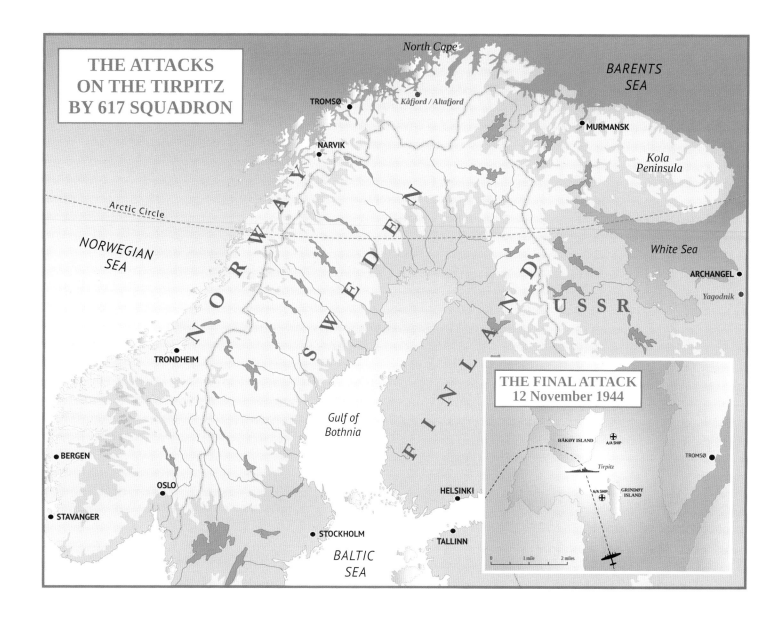

◄ **KNIGHTS MOVE** by Robert Taylor

Tirpitz, in company with the heavy cruisers Admiral Hipper and Admiral Scheer during Operation Rösselsprung, July 1942.

THE ATTACKS ON THE TIRPITZ BY 617 SQUADRON

THE FINAL ATTACK 12 November 1944

KÅFJORD, leading into Altafjord, 200 miles from Tromsö
22 September 1943

The RAF and Fleet Air Arm attacked *Tirpitz* on a regular basis and, in one of her few forays to sea, 12 Fairey Albacores from HMS *Victorious* had launched a daring but unsuccessful torpedo attack. The only serious harm had come not from the air but below the waves when, in an audacious act of bravery for which two submariners received the Victoria Cross, Royal Navy midget submarines penetrated *Tirpitz's* defences at her new moorings in Kåfjord and planted huge mines beneath her hull. The resulting explosions were said to have lifted *Tirpitz* six feet into the air and the damage was enough to put the battleship out of action for the next six months.

However, despite further attacks by carrier-based Barracuda dive-bombers, the Royal Navy, with no further opportunity to sink *Tirpitz* at sea, was unable to sink her from the air. *Tirpitz* was still afloat and the task of slaying Churchill's 'Beast' was finally handed over to Bomber Command. Without hesitation Sir Arthur Harris tasked 617 Squadron and their Tallboys for the job. At the beginning of September 1944, and operating in conjunction with 9 Squadron, they made their first move.

EISMEER PATROL by Anthony Saunders

On one of her few forays to sea, the Tirpitz, escorted by a screening fleet of destroyers and E-boasts and covered by patrolling Fw190s from IV./JG5, begins a voyage north to Bogen to join a large German fleet, including the battleship Scharnhorst and heavy cruiser Lützow, 11 March 1943.

OPERATION SIZILIEN

SPITZBERGEN
8 September 1943

In a move designed to evade the increasingly frequent British bombing raids, the *Tirpitz* left Fættenfjord and Trondheim in March 1943 to join an impressive German battle fleet gathering near Narvik, one of the largest enemy naval bases in Norway, before heading north to Altafjord. And, in September she made a rare appearance at sea: an expedition against a tiny Free Norwegian garrison on Spitzbergen, the only populated island in the Svalbard archipelago far into the Arctic north, and halfway to the Pole. The garrison was defended by two 3-inch guns.

On 6 September the German task force, including *Tirpitz*, the battleship *Scharnhorst* and a flotilla of nine destroyers left Alta and sailed north and, on the morning of 8 September, *Tirpitz* unleashed her guns on the Norwegian positions; it was a one-sided affair – the defenders had two 3-inch guns. The skirmish was soon over. Whilst the Norwegians fell back under fire, German landing parties burnt most of the local buildings to the ground, took a few prisoners and then steamed back to the safety of Altafjord as quickly as they came.

Although her crew could never know it, this brief encounter was not only *Tirpitz's* last operation but the only occasion on which she would ever fire her guns in anger at anything other than aircraft!

YAGODNIK, nr Archangel, Russia
11 September 1944

Tirpitz was still moored in the icy waters of Kåfjord, a spur of Altafjord in remote northern Norway, well within the Arctic Circle; beyond the range of any bomber from Britain to reach and return without refuelling. If the two squadrons were to achieve success the only place from which they could launch an attack was from Russia, and even that would stretch the limits of their heavily-laden Lancasters.

On 11 September 1944 Tait led the force north from Woodall Spa to refuel at Lossiemouth, before heading out on the long trip to a Russian airfield at Yagodnik, just south of Archangel. Here it was planned to refuel, fly west to Kåfjord, bomb *Tirpitz*, and return to Yagodnik before flying back to Britain.

But, as they approached their destination and with fuel running low, the weather closed in. Descending through the cloud base at just 400 feet there was little for the weary crews to see except an expanse of black

forest, lakes and rivers, and the force put down wherever they could. Some found Yagodnik, others found airstrips elsewhere, a few found marshes. Six aircraft were written off but 'Lady Luck' must have been smiling because nobody was killed; but it took several days to reassemble the force and for the weather to clear.

HEROES RETURN by Richard Taylor

Following their successful attack on the Tirpitz, Wg Cdr James Tait (KC-D) and the
Lancasters of 617 Squadron return to RAF Lossiemouth, 12 November 1944.

TARGET BEARING 270° by Robert Taylor

At sunrise on 12 November 1944, Wg Cdr James Tait leads the Lancasters of 617 Squadron in a loose formation as they head out towards their target – the battleship Tirpitz at anchor in a Norwegian fjord.

KÅFJORD, leading into Altafjord, nr Tromsö
15 September 1944

Eventually, on 15 September the weather cleared. Tait was now able to lead the remaining Lancasters away from Yagodnik and head straight for Altafjord. The Germans, however, were quick off the mark; despite attacking from an unsuspected direction, Tait's force was spotted as they climbed to attack. A defensive smoke screen was already beginning to shroud *Tirpitz* as the Lancasters began their run on to the target.

In the nose of Tait's Lancaster his bomb-aimer Danny Daniel had taken a long bead on the fast-disappearing battleship but, by the time he got his bomb away *Tirpitz* was already enveloped. Everyone else, hoping for the best, bombed blind.

One of the other bomb-aimers was sure he had seen Daniel's Tallboy hit the target but it was days before it was confirmed that a Tallboy had struck *Tirpitz's* bows and ripped open her forward deck.

The badly damaged battleship was now moved south to Tromsö Fjord for repair – which just brought her within range of Lossiemouth.

Flying Officer Danny Daniel, the Canadian Bomb-Aimer in Tait's crew:

'We took off from an airfield in Russia to bomb the Tirpitz, in the Altenfjord (now Altafjord) in Norway. This was to be the first of three sorties we made against the Tirpitz.

We took off on 15 September 1944, and approached the target from a direction that surprised the enemy, thus giving us a short advantage. Tait turned our Lancaster on to the bombing run and made a superb run over the target, allowing me to get the battleship beautifully into the cross of my bomb-sights. Just before I released the 6-ton bomb the ship was lost in a smokescreen, however, as we completed our run I saw a terrific explosion,

indicating that we had scored a direct hit. Intelligence reports later told us that we had damaged the Tirpitz so badly that she had to go back to Tromsö for repairs.

After a further unsuccessful attempt to sink her on 29 October – when we arrived (over the target) the cloud was 10/10 – we managed to sink the Tirpitz on 12 November'

TALLBOY ON TARGET
by Richard Taylor

Flying Officer Danny Daniel, Bomb-Aimer in James Tait's Lancaster KC-D, releases their Tallboy during the attack on the Tirpitz, 08.41hrs, 12 November 1944.

Off HÅKØYA ISLAND, TROMSÖ FJORD
09.58 hrs 12 November 1944

This time, as Tait led 617 Squadron, again with 9 Squadron, there was no cloud over Tromsö, no smoke screen and, surprisingly, no enemy fighters. Despite the intense fire from *Tirpitz's* guns, Tallboy after Tallboy rained down from above scoring two direct hits, a near miss and several close by. Holed and listing, it was clear to everyone on board that *Tirpitz* was doomed. At 09.58hrs, rocked by an internal explosion, she finally rolled over and sank. 'The Beast' was no more.

The sinking of the *Tirpitz* was the culmination of Tait's extraordinary spell in command of 617 Squadron. He flew only a few more raids with the squadron until, like Cheshire before him, AVM Cochrane had little choice but to take him off active flying. Tait had completed over 100 operations.

After the raid many thought that, again like Cheshire, Willie Tait should have been awarded the Victoria Cross for his 'sustained gallantry' over nearly five years of continuous operations. Instead he was awarded, alongside his two DFCs, a third bar to his DSO – the only airman ever to be awarded the DSO four times.

As December came to a close Tait handed over command to the tough, determined, no-nonsense Canadian John Emilius 'Johnny' Fauquier, a veteran of two full tours who had volunteered to drop a rank to get the job. Already highly-decorated, Fauquier was known as perhaps the finest bomber pilot in the RCAF and he would now lead the squadron until the last raid of the war.

SINKING THE TIRPITZ by Richard Taylor

Lancaster KC-O, flown by Flight Lieutenant Bob Knights, releases a Tallboy during
617 Squadron's successful attack to sink the German battleship Tirpitz anchored off
Håkøya Island in Tromsö Fjord, 08.42hrs, 12 November 1944.

Designed by Barnes Wallis the 22,000lb 'Grand Slam' was the most powerful conventional bomb of World War II.

ENTER THE GRAND SLAM

The 'Grand Slam' was Wallis's final pièce-de-résistance of the war. It was massive, built to the same design as his Tallboy but longer, wider, heavier and even more deadly than its 'little' brother. The warhead on his new 22,000lb bomb contained over 9,000lbs of Torpex explosive – it was the most powerful conventional bomb of World War II and could only be carried by specially modified Lancasters.

And on 14 March 1945 the first Grand Slam was used in anger for the first time.

ATTACK ON THE VIADUCTS

SCHILDESCHE VIADUCT, BIELEFELD
14 March 1945

The target was the Schildesche viaduct on the line linking Bielefeld to Herford and, for the moment, there were very few Grand Slams – known as 'Special Stores' – ready for use. All of 617 Squadron's Lancasters were carrying Tallboys for this raid, except one, that of Squadron Leader Charles Calder, who was leading the squadron on account of Fauquier's aircraft suffering an engine seizure moments before take-off. Calder's aircraft was carrying the one and only Grand Slam available.

His navigator, Flight Lieutenant John Benison, who had joined the squadron late the previous year 'just as the celebrations at sinking the *Tirpitz* were dying down' recalled:

'With our Lancaster B1 special we had already taken the first 10 ton Grand Slam bomb there the previous day but cloud had obscured the target and we had to bring it back.
We led the Squadron on the day, the other crews having a 12,000lb bomb apiece. As with every crew, the actual bombing was a team effort, the navigator's part being to calculate obscure instrument reading corrections and provide the bomb settings. Bad visibility at the target necessitated last minute changes of plan and frantic calculation of new settings which I had no time to re-check. Result – target demolished!"

Dropped from just under 12,000 feet Calder's Grand Slam, assisted by the Tallboys that followed, had caused over 100 yards of the viaduct to collapse. The spans would take years to rebuild and, luckily, more 'Special Stores' were arriving by the day.

ARNSBERG by Richard Taylor

617 Squadron demolish the strategic railway viaduct across the River Ruhr at Arnsberg, 19 March 1945.

ARNSBERG VIADUCT
19 March 1945

It was perhaps ironic that Arnsberg lay roughly midway between the Möhne dam, a few miles to the north, and the Sorpe dam, two of 617's first ever targets. Now, however, it was the railway viaduct that crossed the River Ruhr at Arnsberg that was to receive the squadron's attention rather than a dam.

Strategically located on a line that directly linked the Ruhr with the centre of Germany, the masonry viaduct remained one of the last crossing points over the river still open to the Germans. It had been attacked repeatedly but still stood, seemingly impervious to destruction. After an unsuccessful attempt in poor visibility on 15 March 1945, four days later 617 returned to finish the job.

The attack was to be carried out by 19 Lancasters, most with Tallboys, but this time the number of Grand Slams available had risen from one to six – all of which were dropped. Together with the Tallboys the bombs blew the structure apart, completely demolishing a huge 40ft span and severely damaging what remained. As far as the Germans were concerned the Arnsberg viaduct would play no further part in the war.

Now, as the supply of Grand Slams increased, so did their use on the raids.

What little remained of Germany's effective infrastructure was steadily removed from the board of play as the endgame was ground out: two large railway bridges in Bremen and another at nearby Nienburg were destroyed over three consecutive days but there were still a few stings in the enemy's tail. One of them was the almost completed submarine plant residing in the largest reinforced concrete bunkers ever built in Germany. The facility was located just north of Bremen and it was to here that 617 turned their attention.

VALENTIN U-BOAT PENS, FARGE
27 March 1945

It was huge, potentially deadly and like many other facilities of war, brutally functional both in design and operation. Situated at Farge, just north of Bremen on the banks of the River Weser which ran into the North Sea 25 miles away, this was not an ordinary U-boat bunker – it was a supposedly bomb-proof ship-building yard designed to withstand anything the Allies could throw at it. Within its walls a fleet of the latest Type XXI

diesel-electric U-boats was about to be assembled from prefabricated parts and rushed into battle.

Construction at Farge had begun in 1943 under the codename Valentin. The finished facility was to be nearly 14,000ft long and over 300ft wide – the equivalent of six

full-size football pitches. Its walls, more than 15ft thick, supported a roof that in part was some 23ft thick, using some of the largest reinforced concrete trusses ever built. It is thought that well over 10,000 slave labourers, mostly housed in a nearby concentration camp, had worked on

LAST GRAND SLAM by Richard Taylor

The final Grand Slam raid of the war was an attack on coastal batteries on Heligoland, 19 April 1945.

Flt Lt Ken Trent's crew gather around their modified Lancaster YZ-A, with a massive Grand Slam bomb slung under the fuselage, in readiness for the successful raid on the Farge U-boat construction bunker, 27 March 1945.

the building and conditions were brutal – some estimate that as many as half the workforce might have died during the construction. Needless to say, members of the SS were never far away.

The Valentin yard was now only days away from completion but if the Kriegsmarine's rapidly diminishing U-boat fleet was hoping for reinforcements out of the new factory, they were going to be disappointed.

On the morning of 27 March, 617 Squadron took off from Woodhall Spa, laid course for Farge and at 13.00hrs they were overhead the bunker to release the first of their earthquake bombs. Where all previous attacks had failed, 617 now succeeded as two Grand Slams scored direct

hits, penetrating part of the massive ferro-concrete roof and, after the delayed-action fuses detonated, brought down thousands of tons of reinforced concrete. The interior of the bunker was shattered, the part-assembled U-boats nothing more than twisted metallic skeletons. Farge, as an operational site, now ceased to exist.

IJMUIDEN, North Holland
7 April 1945

During the previous December, the last raid on which James Tait had led the squadron, 617 had attacked and damaged the substantial E-boat bunkers at Ijmuiden, a port on the north Holland coast from where the Dutch

Royal family had been evacuated by the Royal Navy in May 1940. In February, under Johnny Fauquier, the squadron had returned to finish the job. Now they were going back to Ijmuiden. But this time, with the bunkers already out of action and the German army cut-off, the target of their Tallboys was a flotilla of enemy ships that had slipped through the Allies' blockade.

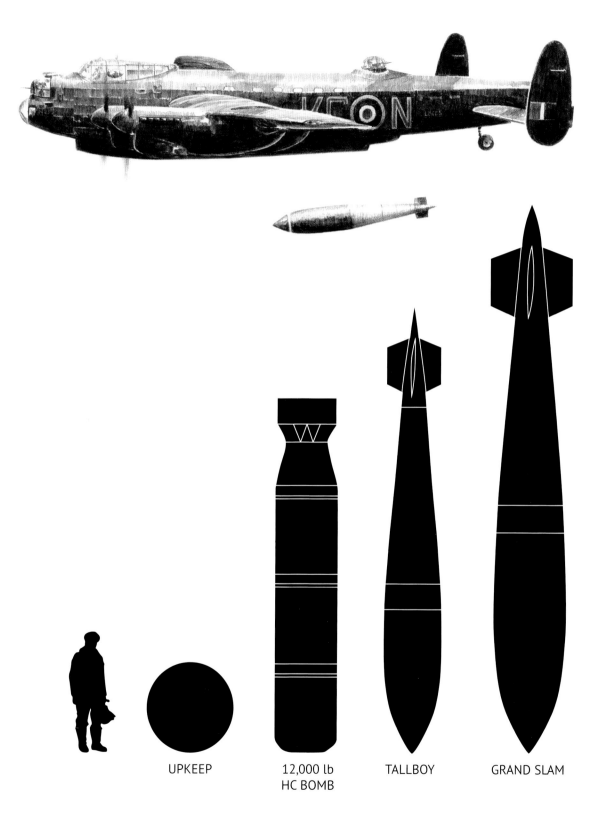

"....MY CONGRATULATIONS ON YOUR ACCURATE BOMBING. YOU HAVE CERTAINLY MADE A PROPER MESS OF IT THIS TIME AND INCIDENTALLY ADDED ANOTHER PAGE TO YOUR HISTORY OF BEING THE FIRST SQUADRON TO DROP THE BIGGEST BOMB ON GERMANY SO FAR...."

From a telegram sent from AVM Ralph Cochrane, AOC 5 Group following 617's attack on the Bielefeld viaduct

THE GREAT BOMBS

UPKEEP

The Bouncing Bomb
Length: 6 ft
Diameter: 60 ins

Weight: 9,250 lbs
Warhead: 6,600 lbs 'Torpex'
(equiv to 3.7 tons of TNT)

12,000 lb HC BOMB

High Capacity Blast Bomb
Length: 16 ft 4 ins
Diameter: 38 ins

Weight: 12,000 lbs
Warhead: 'Torpex' / 'Amatex'
(equiv to 3.8 tons of TNT)

TALLBOY

Deep Penetration Earthquake Bomb
Length: 21 ft
Diameter: 38 ins

Weight: 12,000 lbs
Warhead: 5,200 lbs 'Torpex'
(equiv to 3.7 tons of TNT)

GRAND SLAM

Deep Penetration Earthquake Bomb
Length: 26 ft 6 ins
Diameter: 46 ins

Weight: 22,000 lbs
Warhead: 9,200 lbs 'Torpex'
(equiv to 6.5 tons of TNT)

UPKEEP   12,000 lb   TALLBOY   GRAND SLAM
                HC BOMB

SWINEMÜNDE, Baltic coast
16 April 1945

Two days after the successful Tallboy raid on Ijmuiden, the Grand Slams were back in the mix, this time pulverising the last remaining U-boat pens in Hamburg – a once-great port city now flattened. With the bunkers demolished and the docks in ruins there was little of importance left for the Grand Slams to demolish but, at sea, the last remnants of the Kriegsmarine's surface fleet were still a force to be wary of.

On 16 April, after two aborted attacks due to bad weather, 617 set off to hunt down the heavy cruiser *Prinz Eugen* – veteran survivor of the Bismarck encounter and Operation Cerberus – thought to be in company with another heavy cruiser, the *Lützow*, which was acting as a floating battery in defence of Swinemünde, a port on the Polish Baltic coast where thousands of fleeing Germans were encircled by the advancing Red Army.

Prinz Eugen's charmed luck continued – she escaped, but not so the moored *Lützow* whose hull was torn apart by a near-miss Tallboy and she sank in the shallow waters. The flak, however, had been intense and it was on this raid that 617 suffered their last casualties of the war when the Lancaster of Squadron Leader John Powell DFC was hit and crashed, killing all seven crew.

SPECIAL STORES ▶
by Richard Taylor

Ken Trent releases his Grand Slam to score a direct hit on the U-boat construction bunker at Farge, 27 March 1945.

The Grand Slams would only be used once more when attacking coastal batteries on Heligoland. It was the last operation on which Johnny Fauquier would lead the squadron. As with his predecessor James Tait he had been ordered, much to his dismay, to cease operational flying.

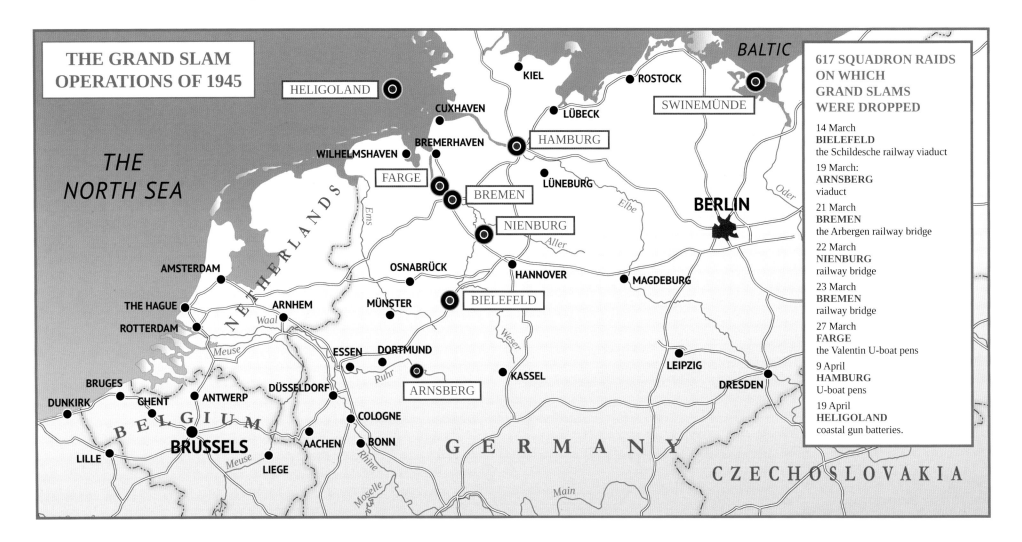

THE GRAND SLAM OPERATIONS OF 1945

THE NORTH SEA

BALTIC

HELIGOLAND

KIEL
ROSTOCK
SWINEMÜNDE
CUXHAVEN
LÜBECK
BREMERHAVEN
HAMBURG
WILHELMSHAVEN
FARGE
LÜNEBURG
BREMEN
Elbe
BERLIN
Oder
NIENBURG
Aller
AMSTERDAM
OSNABRÜCK
HANNOVER
MAGDEBURG
NETHERLANDS
THE HAGUE
ARNHEM
MÜNSTER
BIELEFELD
Waal
Weser
ROTTERDAM
Meuse
ESSEN
DORTMUND
Ruhr
KASSEL
LEIPZIG
BRUGES
ARNSBERG
DRESDEN
DUNKIRK
GHENT
ANTWERP
DÜSSELDORF
COLOGNE
GERMANY
BELGIUM
BRUSSELS
AACHEN
BONN
LILLE
Meuse
LIEGE
Rhine
Moselle
Main
CZECHOSLOVAKIA

617 SQUADRON RAIDS ON WHICH GRAND SLAMS WERE DROPPED

14 March
BIELEFELD
the Schildesche railway viaduct

19 March:
ARNSBERG
viaduct

21 March
BREMEN
the Arbergen railway bridge

22 March
NIENBURG
railway bridge

23 March
BREMEN
railway bridge

27 March
FARGE
the Valentin U-boat pens

9 April
HAMBURG
U-boat pens

19 April
HELIGOLAND
coastal gun batteries.

BERCHTESGADEN

Johnny Fauquier may have been forbidden to fly but 617 Squadron had one final mission to make – to Obersalzberg, Hitler's famed redoubt high in the Bavarian Alps near Berchtesgaden. From this majestic outpost the fates of Poland, France and Russia had been decided, together with the lives of millions.

Now, as the war entered its final days, it was believed that Hitler was cocooned in his fortified bunker in the heart of Berlin, but some in Allied Military Intelligence believed it possible that Hitler might have fled south to his beloved Berchtesgaden and there, surrounded by veterans from his die-hard *Waffen-SS*, made a final Wagnerian stand. If he did so, the battle for Berchtesgaden would be bloody and deadly.

On 25 April 1945, a day when Soviet troops were inching their way through the suburbs towards the Reichstag and the heart of the Berlin, 617 Squadron were issued with their orders: they were to lead the attack on Obersalzberg and obliterate it using their Tallboys. Behind them 400 heavy bombers would follow and finish off anything that survived.

As the sun glints off the mountain peak behind, a pair of Bf109s overfly Hitler's Berghof at Obersalzberg, September 1939.

'These were the best times of my life. My great plans were forged here.'

Adolf Hitler

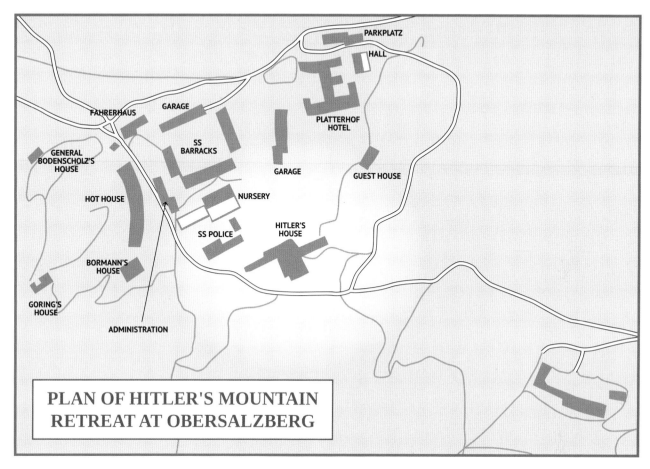

PLAN OF HITLER'S MOUNTAIN RETREAT AT OBERSALZBERG

OBERSALZBERG Berchtesgaden
20 April 1939

Whilst most people find it easy to denounce Hitler's insane vision and demonic morality, few can doubt his taste in choosing Obersalzberg, a small hillside retreat above the town of Berchtesgaden, as the place to build the Berghof – his mountain home.

Just to the south of Salzburg and within easy reach of Munich, the whole area is breathtakingly beautiful, perhaps none more so than Obersalzberg. The Berghof had stunning views across Alpine forests, pastures, lakes and valleys towards the snow-capped mountains of his native Austria. Hitler had fallen in love with the place on his first visit in 1923, travelling under the pseudonym Herr 'Wolf', but later, following his rise to power, he bought a small hillside chalet and began transforming it into an imposing Bavarian country house. This was only the beginning.

Hitler's once-friendly neighbours were forced out of their homes; in their place a new, heavily-fortified outpost of Nazi Government was created: a complex of buildings including offices of state, barracks, guest houses and staff quarters complete with a cinema and school. A labyrinth of tunnels and bunkers was created underground.

Others in the Party leadership were quick to join Hitler in the mountain redoubt: his deputy Hermann Goering and personal aide Martin Bormann built homes within the grounds; Albert Speer, Germany's Minister of Armaments nearby. Josef Goebbels and his family were frequent visitors, as were most of the top Nazi leadership.

There were other guests too. In 1936 the former British Prime Minister David Lloyd George had enjoyed the Führer's hospitality at the Berghof, describing Hitler as 'the greatest German of the age'. The following year the Duke and Duchess of Windsor had also visited, the recently abdicated King believed by some to have greeted the Führer with a Nazi salute. Of the Duchess, Hitler is said to have remarked 'She would have made a very good Queen'.

Chamberlain, too, had visited. The British Prime Minister had been brought here during the 'Munich' crises in 1938, the outcome of which was the unseemly ceding of Czechoslovakia to Germany and a so-called 'peace in our time'.

The one building these important visitors never saw was the Kehisteinhaus – better known as the 'Eagle's Nest'. Perched high on the peak above Obersalzberg, the building was a gift to Hitler from the Nazi Party to celebrate the Führer's 50th birthday. It had taken

In the days following the German surrender, a group of P-51D Mustangs from the 325th Fighter Group – The Checkertails – thunder over the Eagles Nest perched high on a peak above Obersalzberg.

3,000 men to build it, and the only access was by a road blasted up the mountainside to an entrance from where a mirrored brass elevator ascended through 400ft of solid rock to the building above.

OBERSALZBERG Berchtesgaden
25 April 1945

Shortly after 04.00hrs, 617 Squadron thundered away from Woodhall Spa and, together with a force of some 350-odd other aircraft from Bomber Command, set course for the long journey south where, lightly covered with snow, the site around the Berghof awaited its fate.

The 2,000 'residents' crammed into the shelters as the ground shook. Four Tallboys annihilated the SS barracks, the Berghof was pummelled and the fine houses created by Goering and Bormann reduced to ruins, as were targets in the town of Berchestgaden below.

Only the Eagle's Nest escaped the damage and destruction, unprepared for the curious eyes of advancing US and French troops.

Five days after the raid Hitler, still in his bunker in Berlin, committed suicide. On Tuesday 8 May 1945 representatives of the German High Command signed the Unconditional Instrument of Surrender. The war in Europe was over.

Japan, however, was still fighting.

BERGHOF DESTROYED
by Richard Taylor

Troops from the US 101st Airborne on the approach to the wrecked remains of Hitler's Berghof, May 1945.

PART FIVE
MISSION COMPLETED

BERLIN
Tuesday 8 May 1945

The unconditional surrender of all German forces, signed in Berlin on 8 May 1945, brought the war in Europe to an end. Although the fighting was over, the flying was not and the immediate task for 617 was their participation in Operation Exodus – the mass repatriation of newly liberated Allied prisoners of war.

In the Far East, however, an increasingly bloody and bitter war against the Japanese was far from over. The closer the fighting came to Japan, the more fanatical had been the resistance: the battle to take Iwo Jima had cost over 26,000 US Marine casualties and, on the day that Germany surrendered, the Marines were engaged in a desperate fight to capture Okinawa, less than 400 miles south of mainland Japan.

Okinawa was the island from which the planned Allied invasion of Japan, scheduled for January 1946, could be launched, and the plans called for Bomber Command to assemble 22 squadrons of long-range heavy bombers and dispatch them to Okinawa as what was to be known as 'Tiger Force'.

With their specialist experience with Tallboys and Grand Slams, 617 were prime candidates for inclusion and they soon found themselves moving away from Woodhall Spa to nearby RAF Waddington in readiness for the forthcoming and somewhat daunting trip to Okinawa. The preparations included the receipt of new Lancasters complete with a new paint scheme: the Lancasters' upper surfaces resplendent in white – supposedly to reflect heat from the expected harsh sunlight, and the under surfaces black.

The squadron never got to Okinawa. Shortly after 08.00hrs on the morning of 6 August 1945, the Americans dropped an atomic bomb from the B-29 *Enola Gay* over Hiroshima. It detonated 2,000ft above the city and, in the blink of an eye, history witnessed the first target to be obliterated by an atomic weapon fired in anger. Three days later another bomb fell on Nagasaki.

The Japanese had no option but to surrender. On 15 August 1945 Emperor Hirohito made the announcement in a radio address to the nation which was ratified on 2 September by the formal signing of the Instrument of Surrender on the deck of the battleship USS *Missouri* anchored in Tokyo Bay. Although the effects and suffering would be felt for years, the most costly war in human history was officially at an end.

◄ **MISSION COMPLETED** by Simon Smith

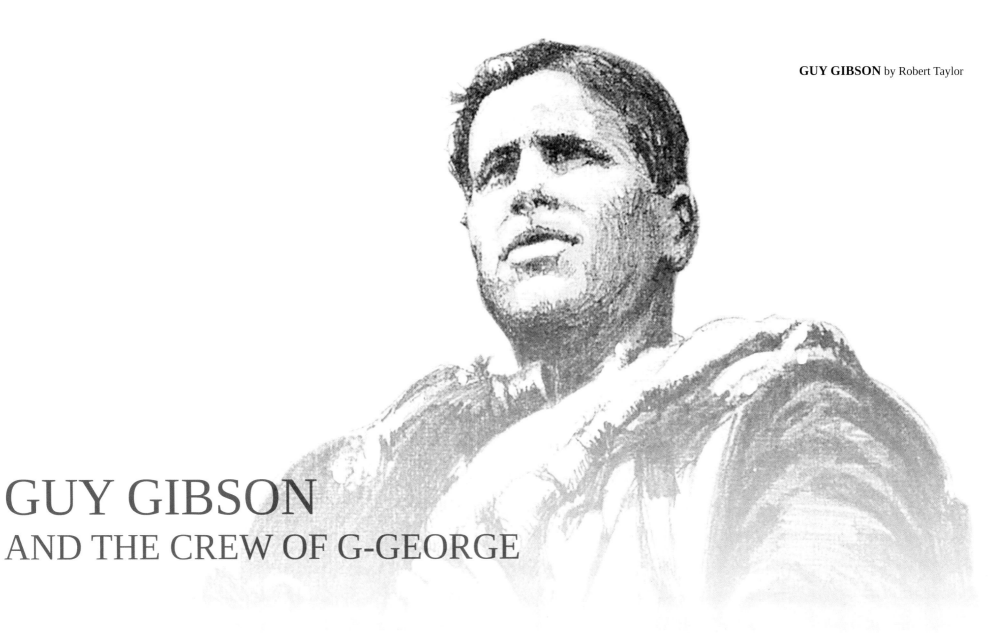

GUY GIBSON
AND THE CREW OF G-GEORGE

STEENBERGEN Holland
19 September 1944

The fame that the war had brought 617 was counter-balanced by the tragedy of the many young men who had died flying with the squadron. Of the 80 airmen who survived Operation Chastise, including the three who were taken as PoWs, less than 50 would live to see the end of the war; the others would perish either while serving with 617 in later operations, or in other squadrons.

Amongst them was Guy Gibson. Having relinquished command and been taken off flying, Gibson, with a Victoria Cross now added to his many decorations, became a well-known personality and spent time on goodwill tours, boosting morale in both the UK and USA. The glamour of his celebrity status increasing further after he wrote *Enemy Coast Ahead*, an enthralling account of his wartime bomber experiences, which became an instant but in the event, posthumous best-seller.

Because Gibson was determined to return to the fight once more, eventually his tenacity and relentless requests were rewarded. His wish was granted, albeit reluctantly, and he was given permission to fly one more mission – as a Master Bomber on a raid to Rheydt and

Mönchengladbach and not far from his old 617 stomping ground – the Ruhr.

It was to prove a fatal decision. Returning from the raid at the controls of a Mosquito from 627 Squadron, he and his navigator, Squadron Leader Jim Warwick, were killed when their aircraft crashed in Holland. The Dambuster hero is buried alongside his navigator close to where they crashed at Steenbergen.

None of Gibson's crew on Operation Chastise were to survive the war either: Terry Taerum the navigator, Bob Hutchison the wireless operator, bomb-aimer Spam Spafford and front gunner George Deering had continued to fly with Gibson's successor George Holden. They all died alongside their new CO on the night of 15 / 16 September 1943 during the disastrous Dortmund-Ems canal raid.

Flight Engineer Sgt John Pulford was killed in February 1944 when the Lancaster in which he was flying crashed into the Sussex Downs in heavy fog.

Original drawing by Robert Taylor

FINAL SORTIE by Richard Taylor

With his request to fly one last mission granted, Guy Gibson teams up with navigator Jim Warwick to fly a Mosquito from 627 Squadron and act as Master Bomber for a raid to Rheydt and Mönchengladbach on 19 September 1944. Returning home, however, he and his navigator were killed when their aircraft crashed in Holland.

SCAMPTON FAREWELL by Richard Taylor

Guy Gibson and his crew take a last look at Scampton airfield before climbing aboard
Lancaster G-George at the start of Operation Chastise, 16 May 1943.

Squadron Leader Bill Suggitt's crew had recently landed along with the rest of 617 at nearby RAF Ford after an attack on the Antheor viaduct in southern France and were now returning on the short hop to Lincolnshire. All the crew died along with intelligence officer Squadron Leader Tommy Lloyd.

Lloyd, a decorated veteran of the First World War, was 52 years old and 617's Intelligence Officer. Having debriefed the crews, Suggitt offered him a ride back to Woodall Spa, with fateful consequences.

The last of Gibson's Chastise crew to be killed was the tall rear gunner, Richard Trevor-Roper, who had elected not to join Holden's crew. Instead he joined 97 Squadron but was killed on the night of 30 / 31 March 1944 when his aircraft was shot down on Bomber Command's most costly raid of the war – the attack on Nuremberg in which 95 bombers, including Trevor-Roper's, were lost.

IN MEMORIAM by Richard Taylor ▶

AVRO LINCOLN by Simon Smith

In September 1946, 617 Squadron re-equipped with the
Lancaster's long-awaited successor – the Lincoln.

THE LEGACY

By September 1946 the days of its much-loved
Lancasters were over and the squadron re-equipped
with the long-awaited successor – the Avro Lincoln, in
which they undertook a two-month 'goodwill' tour of the
United States and Canada. In the process they completed
one of the first transatlantic crossings made by a squadron
en masse. It took them 11 hours and 45 minutes.

But the days of piston-engine bombers were
drawing to a close as jet technology, part-inspired by the
Luftwaffe's revolutionary Me262, quickly gave birth
to the first generation jet bombers. Among them was
the stylish English Electric Canberra, which 617 took
possession of in January 1952 and later flew in pride

of place during the flypast over Buckingham Palace to
celebrate the Coronation of Queen Elizabeth II.

It had been ten years since 617 Squadron had
seen action but, in 1955, they and their Canberras
were deployed to the Far East, successfully attacking
communist guerrillas in the Malayan Emergency. It was
a short-lived campaign and, returning home, they found
that they were to be disbanded with the intention of their
becoming the RAF's first Vulcan squadron – although
that honour eventually went to 83 Squadron.

In 1958, after a major upgrade that included a
new, lengthened runway, 617's old haunt at Scampton
was re-opened to accommodate part of the RAF's new

V-bomber force and the squadron was re-formed – the
first to be equipped with the Avro Vulcan armed with
Britain's nuclear bomb. It was the role they carried out
until the responsibility for Britain's nuclear deterrent was
transferred to Royal Navy.

On 16 May 1983, forty years to the day after the
predecessors had set out on Operation Chastise, 617
Squadron were back in the low-level, precision-bombing
business. Operating out of RAF Marham in Norfolk, they
now became operational on the swing-wing Tornado.
Ironically it had been none other than Barnes Wallis who
had originally developed the mechanics of swing-wing

AVRO VULCAN
by Richard Taylor

617 reformed at Scampton in 1958 – the first squadron to be equipped with the Avro Vulcan armed with Britain's nuclear bomb.

TORNADO
by Richard Taylor

The Diamond Jubilee of 617 Squadron's formation saw the unit's Tornados in action during the invasion of Iraq, 2003.

aircraft but, lacking official support, his designs were used by the Americans.

The Tornado was specifically designed to strike targets behind enemy lines – a feature that 617 put to good use, helping to remove Saddam Hussein from Kuwait in 1990 followed by the Gulf War a year later.

In 1994 the squadron moved away from Marham to Lossiemouth, the base they had last visited back in 1944 en-route to sink the *Tirpitz*. And now, after distinguished service in Afghanistan, what of the future?

Whatever it holds, the RAF can be sure of one thing: the legend of the 'Dam Busters' will always live on.

UNSUNG HEROES by Richard Taylor

During the afternoon of 16 May 1943 ground crew at Scampton worked tirelessly to load all the Upkeep bombs onto 617's specially modified Lancasters in readiness for Operation Chastise.

ACKNOWLEDGEMENTS

CREATED BY THE MILITARY GALLERY

With special thanks to our production team:

Written by Michael Craig
Production Manager: Craig Smith
Typesetting and Design: Ingrid Freeman
Coordinators: Penny Stratton & Rod Tepesano

We wish to extend our thanks to Dr Robert Owen, Official Historian of 617 Squadron Association and a Trustee of the Barnes Wallis Foundation for his help in the compilation of this book. Membership of the 617 Squadron Association is open to all current and former members of 617 Squadron since its formation in 1943. The Barnes Wallis Foundation aims to inspire, to inform, and to educate a wide audience across fields that Sir Barnes Wallis had embodied through his work, or were otherwise dear to him.
www.barneswallisfoundation.co.uk

Our thanks also to author and historian Jonathan Falconer.

Where not otherwise cited, all other permissions are courtesy of the Military Gallery.

Published by Griffon International Ltd

Printed in China

Many of the images featured in this book have been reproduced as limited edition prints by the Military Gallery.

www.militarygallery.com

BIBLIOGRAPHY:

Printed:

After The Flood by John Nichol (William Collins 2015)
Enemy Coast Ahead by Guy Gibson (Crécy Publishing 2001)
Bomber Pilot by Leonard Cheshire V.C. (Mayflower 1975)
Bomber Squadrons of the RAF by Philip Moyes (McDonald 1964)
Living With Heroes by Harry Humphries (Erskine Press 2003)
Lower Than Low by Tom Simpson (Libra Books Tasmania 1995)
The Men Who Breached The Dams by Alan W. Cooper (William Kimber 1983)
The Dam Busters by Paul Brickhill (Pan Books 1954)
The Dam Busters by Jonathan Falconer (Stroud Publishing Ltd. 2003)
The Dambusters Raid by John Sweetman (Cassell Military Paperbacks 2003)
The Last British Dambuster by George 'Johnny' Johnson (Ebury Press 2014)

Online:

www.raf.mod.uk / www.rafmuseum.org.uk / www.historyofwar.org
www.iwm.org.uk / Peter Schelebaum – www.go2war2.nl
www.bombercommandmuseum.ca / www.v2rocket.com
www.wikipedia.org